Everyday Science and Technology

—News You Can Use—

Jim Knudsen

annotated by Yukinobu Satake

NAN'UN-DO

Download Audio

音声ファイル
無料 DL
のご案内

このテキストの音声を無料で視聴（ストリーミング）・ダウンロードできます。自習用音声としてご活用ください。
以下のサイトにアクセスしてテキスト番号で検索してください。

https://nanun-do.com　テキスト番号［**512204**］

※ 無線 LAN（WiFi）に接続してのご利用を推奨いたします。

※ 音声ダウンロードは Zip ファイルでの提供になります。
お使いの機器によっては別途ソフトウェア（アプリケーション）の導入が必要となります。

Read by

Shizuka Anderson
Ryan Drees

※ Everyday Science and Technology 音声ダウンロードページは以下の QR コードからもご利用になれます。

To the Students

We live in what some have dubbed "The Age of Science and Technology." More and more, our lives and societies are being affected (some would say for better or worse) by momentous discoveries in every scientific field and by advances in every area of technology—progress that purports, even promises, to make life better and easier for everyone (though there is some doubt and controversy about such claims). This textbook—*Everyday Science and Technology*—takes a brief, popular-science look at some recent key breakthroughs, game-changing inventions, and salient trends.

I am not a scientist or technologist by any means, but I am fascinated by the many science-and-technology news stories that I read and hear about every day. In this textbook, I wanted to share some of that fascination with you. The book's subtitle—"News You Can Use"—suggests what I see as perhaps the text's primary benefit. I have come up with stories and information that I think will be useful to you—news that will increase your understanding and appreciation of (and perhaps concern about) life and society today, but at the same time will give you essential facts and ideas that will help you navigate your way through and thrive in our always exciting but also challenging period of history.

But of course *Everyday Science and Technology* is first and foremost an English textbook—one that I have tried to make easy, straightforward, and a pleasure to use. There are 15 units or lessons, each with a reading of 300-350 words written in natural, everyday English—some of it necessarily technical but always presented in an accessible, reader-friendly way so as not to overwhelm or discourage. The follow-up comprehension and vocabulary-study activities are all designed not to test you but to help you get the most out of each reading and allow you to retain the "news you can use" offered in it. Each unit ends with a listening activity related to the reading's main topic.

All in all, *Everyday Science and Technology* will give you an excellent workout—a challenging but effective language-fitness program that will build up your stock of knowledge, strengthen all your English skills, boost your confidence, and, I hope, spark your awe and curiosity about our wonderful (but also anxious) world of everyday science and technology.

NOTE: The information in this textbook was gleaned from many science-news sources in the public domain, including *ScienceDaily*, *LiveScience*, *ScienceNews*, *STAT*, *Yahoo News*, *Reuters*, and *Associated Press*.

CONTENTS

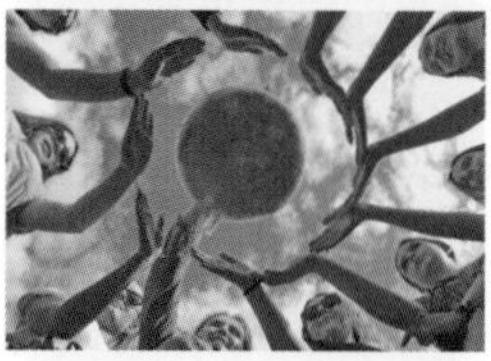

Lesson 1

Artificial Intelligence

AI's Impact on Art

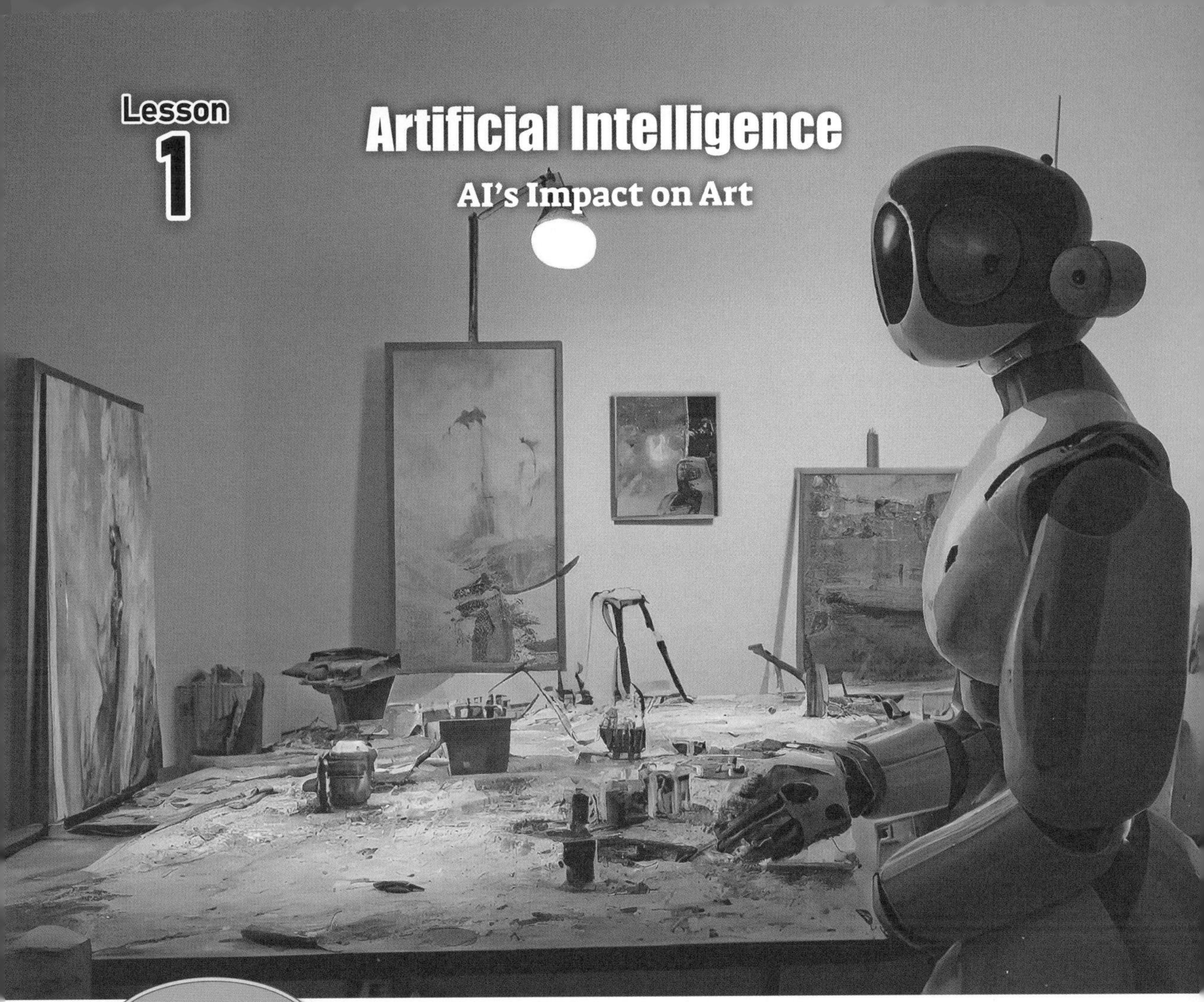

Looking Ahead

As you read today's reading on the next page, look for answers to these questions.

1. Why does it sometimes seem as if AI is "taking over the world"?
2. What can AI's and robots do better and faster than humans?
3. What can AI art tools now produce?
4. What do art AI's have in their data bases?
5. Why are ad-agency creators especially pleased with AI art?
6. What does Aimee Cozza say that AI art does NOT require?
7. What do "real" artists especially dislike about AI art?

Part 1 Reading:
Read the essay below and do the activities that follow. DL 02

[1] Today, it can seem as if AI—**artificial** intelligence—is taking over the world. From shopping to dating, schools to gaming, factories to farms, AI technology is transforming nearly every aspect of modern life. It's easy to see why. AI robots can turn out more of every **commodity** in far less time than **conventional** production methods. They can examine data far faster than any human. They accomplish all this cheaply and efficiently, without fatigue or boredom, and nearly error-free.

[2] Advances in AI are also having an impact on art. Special AI art tools can now produce paintings, photographs, and many other artworks. They allow us to create almost anything we can imagine. "Type in a few words, and up pops an **assortment** of artistic images," says digital artist Aimee Cozza.

[3] Of course, it's not quite that simple. The "few words" we type in are actually a short **description** of the painting or sculpture we have in our mind's eye. AI Art has a huge collection of pictures in its data base. They search through all these images and recognize patterns among them. This allows them to **eventually** come up with artworks that match the descriptions we have given them.

[4] To the average person, this is a dream come true. Almost anyone can now create art, "without doing all the studying and practice and hard work to get good at it," says Aimee Cozza. Creative workers such as ad-agency illustrators are especially happy with the technology. AI art shows them almost **immediately** what the great new idea they are picturing in their imaginations will actually look like.

[5] But not everyone is a fan of AI art. Many "legitimate" artists are put off by it. It's totally unfair, they complain. They **resent** having to compete against computers for attention, jobs, and art prizes. "It's hard," adds Aimee Cozza, "for artists. They hate to see people who have never picked up a pencil make nice things using just a simple, typed-in description and borrowed art styles. It's even harder when they see people acting as if they've made the art with their own skilled hands."

Notes turn out：生産する / accomplish：成し遂げる / boredom：退屈 / up pops = pops up：突然現れる、ポンと飛び上がる / sculpture：彫刻 / come up with：～を思いつく / match：～に合致する / ad agency：広告代理店 / picture：描く / legitimate：本物の、真の / put off：うんざりさせる / complain：不平を言う / compete against：～と争う、競う

Part 2 Comprehension:
Follow the instructions for each activity below.

A *Choose the correct answer.*

1. Which of these fields is NOT mentioned as one way in which artificial intelligence—AI—is transforming modern life?
   a. health and medicine b. education c. agriculture
2. What does paragraph 1 say that AI robots can do faster than any human?
   a. produce goods b. analyze information c. play games
3. The underlined word "fatigue" in paragraph 1 refers to people's
   a. being tired. b. getting old. c. needing help.

B *Circle T if the sentence is true, F if it is false.*

4. T F Paintings and photos are the only artworks AI art tools can produce.
5. T F Aimee Cozza designs computers for a living.
6. T F The underlined phrase "mind's eye" in paragraph 3 is a synonym for "imagination."

C *Fill in the blanks in the sentences below. Listen to check your answers.* DL 03

7. The "few words" Aimee Cozza mentions are actually a ________________ of the artwork we want to create.
8. An AI art ________________ is filled with a huge ________________ of images or pictures.
9. To most people, including creative people like ________________, AI art is like a dream come ________________.
10. "________________" artists complain that AI art is totally ________________.

D ***Writing Challenge:*** *Write a full-sentence answer to each question below. Listen to check your answers.* DL 04

11. What do people who create AI art NOT have to do, according to Aimee Cozza?

____

____

12. What does Aimee Cozza say especially upsets "real" artists about people who make AI art, even though those people have never picked up a pencil?

____

____

Part 3 Vocabulary Study: Follow the instructions for each activity below.

A *Match these KEY WORDS from today's reading with the definitions and synonyms below. Write the words on the lines. (The words are highlighted in bold in the reading.)*

artificial	assortment	commodity	conventional
description	eventually	immediately	resent

1. ______________ product or good; material thing
2. ______________ over time; after a while; someday
3. ______________ false; imitation; not real
4. ______________ a picture in words; sketch; depiction
5. ______________ to be angry about; feel bitter; begrudge
6. ______________ variety; range; selection
7. ______________ right away; very soon
8. ______________ traditional; normal; ordinary; old-fashioned

B *Fill in the blank in each sentence below with the correct form of one of these words to make a phrasal verb (idiom) used in today's reading. Listen to check your answers. (The meaning of the phrase is shown in brackets after each sentence.)*

DL 05

come	pop	take	turn

1. This new machine can ____________ **out** 500 sandwiches per hour. [make]
2. Can you help me ____________ **up with** a name for our new robot? [create]
3. Gerald always tries to ____________ **over** our meetings. He's really rude. [control]
4. So many ads ____________ **up** on my computer. How can I stop them? [appear]

Part 4 Listening Challenge: Listen to the short talk. Then circle T if each sentence below is true, or F if it is false.

DL 06

1. T F ChatGPT is the only chatbot that has so far been created.
2. T F ChatGPT came out in November 2023.
3. T F ChatGPT uses AI to produce text.
4. T F ChatGPT's language is similar to how people speak and write.
5. T F ChatGPT is not at all useful in mathematics.
6. T F ChatGPT is difficult for the average person to use.
7. T F ChatGPT's information for its responses is gathered from the internet.
8. T F ChatGPT might cause some students to use it to do all their schoolwork.

Lesson 2

Ecology/Environmental Science (1)

Solar Geoengineering

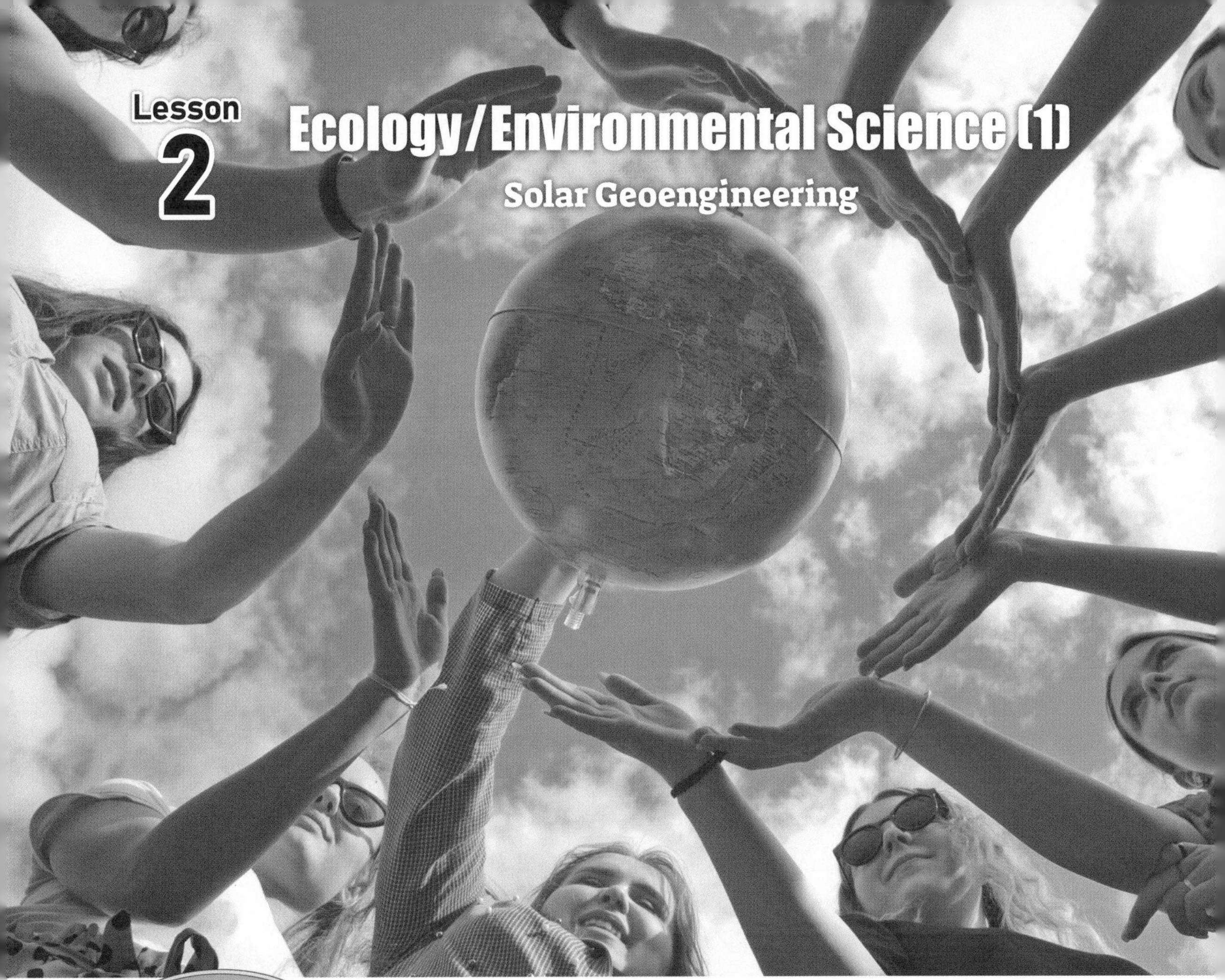

Looking Ahead

As you read today's reading on the next page, look for answers to these questions.

1. What will happen if we don't take action to slow global warming?
2. What is geoengineering, and what does it aim to do?
3. What are two geoengineering methods?
4. What are three types of solar geoengineering?
5. What did a recent Harvard study show about solar engineering?
6. Why do some scientists oppose solar engineering?
7. What do these scientists say we should do about climate change?

Part 1 Reading:

Read the essay below and answer the questions that follow. DL 07

[1] Global warming is **accelerating** every year. If we don't take **drastic** action very soon, say most climate scientists and environmentalists, Earth and every living being on it will be lost forever.

[2] To **avoid** this sad future, some scientists are putting forth geoengineering as a course of action. Geoengineering refers to large-scale methods for changing Earth's climate. One such technique calls for removing excess heat-causing carbon dioxide from the atmosphere. This would be carried out by reforestation (planting millions of trees around the globe) or by adopting "carbon capture technology" (completely removing carbon **emissions** from car and factory exhaust). But the former will take far too long, and the latter is still far from ready for everyday use.

[3] Another option is solar geoengineering. There are three possible methods involved. One method is to put aerosol sprays into the atmosphere. Another is to make clouds whiter by spraying them with seawater. The other **option** is to thin out the thick cirrus clouds that trap the sun's heat close to Earth's surface. All of these methods aim to cool Earth's surface by deflecting sunlight away from it.

[4] In theory at least, all these technologies could slow global warming cheaply and, better yet, quickly. But perhaps not just in theory. A recent Harvard agricultural research project created a promising model. The researchers concluded that spraying aerosols into the atmosphere will definitely help protect farm crops. Many scientists now say that this and other similar studies show that we need to start taking solar geoengineering very seriously—before it's too late.

[5] Nevertheless, many other scientists oppose solar geoengineering. It is too **risky**, they say. No one knows for certain what the consequences of "messing with" nature will be. What if it is more damaging than climate change itself? To these critics, solar geoengineering is a **superficial**, "quick-fix" solution. It doesn't get to the root of our problems. They even recommend that all basic research into solar geoengineering be called off. Their biggest concern, however, is that if geoengineering becomes a more accepted practice, we will rely too much on it. And if we do that, we will give up trying to find better ways to truly—and permanently—curb global warming.

Notes put forth：～を提出する、発表する / geoengineering：地球工学 / a course of action：一連の措置 / large-scale：大規模な / call for：～を必要とする / remove A from B：A を B から取り除く / excess：過度の、余分の / carbon dioxide：二酸化炭素 / carry out：実施する / reforestation：植林 / adopt：採用する / capture：捕らえること / exhaust：排出ガス / far from：少しも～でない / surface：表面 / deflect：逸らす / aerosol：エアゾール / spray：～に［しぶきなどを］かける［with］/ thin out：希薄にする / cirrus cloud：巻雲 / agricultural：農業の、農学の / consequence：結果 / mess with：をもてあそぶ / quick-fix：急場しのぎの、間に合わせの / concern：心配、懸念 / curb：抑制する

Part 2 Comprehension:
Follow the instructions for each activity below.

A *Choose the correct answer.*

1. The phrase "lost forever" as used in paragraph 1 is closest in meaning to
   a. slightly damaged. b. completely destroyed. c. hiding out.
2. Which of these is NOT a purpose or goal of geoengineering?
   a. to change Earth's weather b. to please some scientists
   c. to save Earth from a sad future
3. Why do we need to remove carbon dioxide from the atmosphere?
   a. We do not have enough of it. b. It has a bad smell.
   c. It is a cause of global warming and climate change.

B *Circle T if the sentence is true, F if it is false.*

4. T F Reforestation cannot be done quickly.
5. T F The word "exhaust" is a synonym for "gasoline."
6. T F "Carbon capture technology" is still being developed.

C *Fill in the blanks in the sentences below. Listen to check your answers.* DL 08

7. One solar geoengineering method is to spray ________________ into Earth's ________________.
8. ________________ clouds are very ________________, which is why they trap the sun's heat close to Earth's ________________.
9. The Harvard study had to do with ________________ and why solar geoengineering might help protect farm ________________.
10. Some scientists say that solar geoengineering is a "________________" solution that doesn't get to the ________________ of the global-warming problem.

D ***Writing Challenge:*** *Write a full-sentence answer to each question below. Listen to check your answers.* DL 09

11. What do all three of the solar geoengineering methods mentioned in paragraph 3 have as their main aim or goal?

____

12. What do some scientists worry might happen if solar engineering becomes an accepted method?

____

Part 3 Vocabulary Study: Follow the instructions for each activity below.

A *Fill in the blank in each sentence-definition or description below with one of these words. (The words are highlighted in bold in the reading.)*

accelerate	avoid	consequence	drastic
emissions	option	risky	superficial

1. A ______________ is a result or effect, often a bad or negative one.
2. Something that is ______________ is not deep. It is shallow, in other words.
3. When a car begins to ______________, it goes faster.
4. A very serious situation is a ______________ or dramatic situation.
5. Exhaust ______________ are the smoke and smells coming from cars and factories.
6. When we ______________ a job or duty, we stay away from it and don't do it.
7. A ______________ adventure is one that involves some danger.
8. An ______________ is a choice that you can or have to make.

B *Fill in the blank in each sentence below with one of these prepositions to make a phrasal verb (idiom) used in today's reading. Listen to check your answers. (The meaning of the phrase is shown in brackets after each sentence.)*

DL 10

for	forth	off	out

1. The idea for the video game was **put** ________ by a student. [propose, suggest]
2. This technique **calls** ________ great skill and patience. [require, demand]
3. The test was **carried** ________ by researchers at Harvard University. [do, perform]
4. The conference was **called** ________ because of COVID-19. [cancel]

Part 4 Listening Challenge: As you listen to the short talk, fill in the blank(s) in each sentence below. Listen to check your answers.

DL 11

1. The test took place on __________________ in 2022.
2. It wasn't an example of ________________ or a way to cool Earth's ________________.
3. An asteroid is a kind of space __________________.
4. In the test, a spacecraft __________________ into an asteroid called Dimorphos.
5. The test was no __________________. It was part of NASA's "planetary defense __________________."
6. The test was successful because the spacecraft hit its __________________.
7. In the future, we now will know how to change an asteroid's __________________.
8. We can stop the asteroid from crashing into Earth and causing great __________________.

Lesson 3

Archeology/Anthropology

Recycling: Older Than You Think

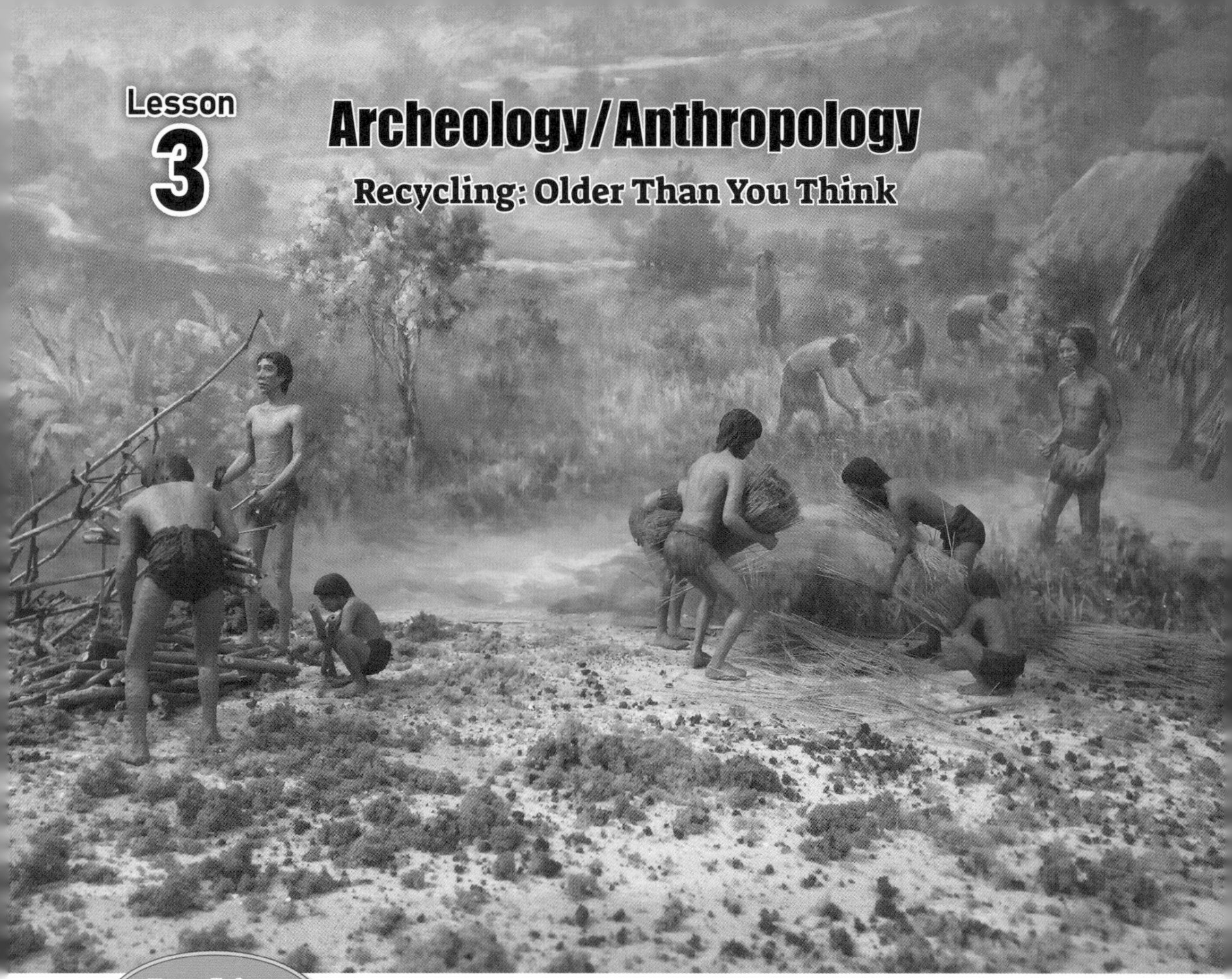

Looking Ahead

As you read today's reading on the next page, look for answers to these questions.

1. What do we "modern" people believe about our recycling?
2. Some 400,000 years go, what were our ancient ancestors doing?
3. What kind of conference was held recently, and where?
4. How did early humans see artifacts that had been made by their ancestors?
5. Where was some important archeological evidence found?
6. What did Professor Ari Gopher have to say about ancient people's recycling?
7. What story does Professor Ran Barkai tell about ancient people's recycling?

Part 1 Reading:

Read the essay below and do the activities that follow.

DL 12

[1] We "moderns" often think that recycling is new. We are prone to believe that we became more **conscious** of the need for "recycling, reducing, and reusing" only recently. But several new studies show that that is not the case. Over 400,000 years ago, our prehistoric ancestors were already recycling tools that had been made and used by their **predecessors**. But they didn't do this out of **concern** for the environment alone. So what did drive them?

[2] A recent archeology conference held in Tel Aviv, Israel, came up with a surprising explanation: Early humans practiced recycling because they saw personal and cultural meaning in the artifacts of their forebears. They regarded the objects as nostalgic—as something valuable that needed saving.

[3] "Recycling was a way of life for these people," Professor Ran Barkai told Yahoo News. Archeological evidence found in Israel's Qesem Cave shows that they regularly recycled **discarded** tools made of a rock called flint. From this tool, they created small, sharp tools of their own that they used for all kinds of daily **tasks**.

[4] Evidently, ancient humans recycled old objects for the same reason that we do today—for the sake of **efficiency**. "Recycling an old flint tool meant that you didn't have to go back to the rock quarry to dig out more flint," explained Professor Ari Gopher. "In that way, you saved resources and **conserved** energy."

[5] That, however, wasn't early humans' only motivation. Ran Barkai explains the ancients' behavior something like this: "Imagine you are a stone age man walking through the forest. You spot an old flint tool lying on the ground. It somehow means something to you. Perhaps it carries the memory of your ancestors. Or maybe it reminds you of a place that has special meaning to you. You pick the artifact up and weigh it in your hands. It pleases you, so you take it back to your cave. A gut feeling tells you that using it every day will keep your fond memory alive. So you make it into a new but similar tool. You do this not only because it will be **practical**. You also do it out of respect for the original maker. In this way, just as we do today, our ancestors preserved artifacts to bond with older worlds."

Notes be prone to：～しがちである、傾向のある / case：事実、実情 / prehistoric：有史以前の / ancestor：先祖 / archeology：考古学 / conference：会議 / Tel Aviv：テルアビブ（イスラエルの都市） / artifact：人工の物 / forebear：先祖 / object：物 / Qesem Cave：ケセム洞窟 / flint：燧石 / quarry：石切り場 / somehow：どういうわけか / weigh：（手にもって）の重さを見る / gut feeling：勘

Part 2 Comprehension:
Follow the instructions for each activity below.

A *Choose the correct answer.*

1. Which of these is true?
   a. Recycling is older than we moderns think.
   b. Recycling is a recent, modern practice.
   c. Our ancestors only cared about protecting nature.

2. The findings of an archeology conference held in Tel Aviv, Israel, were
   a. as expected. b. a disappointment. c. unexpected.

3. It can be reasonably inferred that Ran Barkai
   a. is an archeologist. b. lives in Tel Aviv.
   c. is the person who found the evidence.

B *Circle T if the sentence is true, F if it is false.*

4. T F "Flint" is a special tool used by ancient people.
5. T F Ancient people used the tools they made for various purposes.
6. T F Recycling old tools saves resources.

C *Fill in the numbered blanks in the short paragraph below based on Ran Barkai's story. Listen to check your answers.* DL 13

Imagine you are a (7)______________ man walking through the forest. You spot an old flint tool lying on the ground. It somehow means something to you. Perhaps it carries the (8)______________ of your (9)______________. Or maybe it reminds you of a place that has special meaning to you. You pick the (10)______________ up, weigh it in your hands. It pleases you, so you take it back to your cave.

D ***Writing Challenge:*** *Write a full-sentence answer to each question below. Listen to check your answers.* DL 14

11. According to Ari Gopher, what did recycling mean to ancient people?

____

12. According to Ran Barkai, fashioning (making) a new tool from an old one had more than just a practical purpose. What else did preserving artifacts do?

____

Part 3 Vocabulary Study: Follow the instructions for each activity below.

A *Match these KEY WORDS from today's reading with the definitions and synonyms below. Write the words on the lines. (The words are highlighted in bold in the reading.)*

concern	conscious	conserve	discarded
efficiency	practical	predecessor	task

1. ______________________ aware of; thinking about; awake
2. ______________________ for everyday use; useful; pragmatic; functional
3. ______________________ thrown away; tossed out; no longer in use
4. ______________________ someone who comes before someone else
5. ______________________ a piece of work to be done; small job; chore
6. ______________________ to save; protect; preserve; sustain
7. ______________________ a worry; a matter of interest or importance
8. ______________________ effectiveness; saving time, energy, or money

B *Rewrite each sentence below by substituting one of these phrases for the underlined part. Make the necessary changes. Listen to check your answers.* DL 15

the case	call to mind	all kinds of	prone to

1. This old toy <u>makes me remember</u> my childhood.

____

2. What you are saying is simply not <u>true</u>.

____

3. You <u>tend to use</u> too many difficult words in your writing.

____

4. This museum has <u>many different</u> ancient artifacts on display.

____

Part 4 Listening Challenge: Listen to the short talk. Then write a short answer to each question you hear. DL 16

1. ____
2. ____
3. ____
4. ____
5. ____
6. ____

Lesson 4

Criminology/Sociology/Psychology

Safety in Green

Looking Ahead

As you read today's reading on the next page, look for answers to these questions.

1. What is "psychopathy"?
2. What do psychologists and sociologists think causes crime?
3. What insights do criminologists use in their studies?
4. How many cities were used in a recent study of urban crime?
5. What are some examples of "property crimes"?
6. What are some examples of "violent crimes"?
7. What was the surprising but hopeful finding of a recent study of criminal behavior?

Part 1 Reading:

Read the essay below and do the activities that follow. DL 17

[1] Crime—in particular **urban** crime—has many causes. Different social scientists have different ideas about what those causes are. Psychologists usually cite problems related to character and personality. One extreme example is "psychopathy." People with this illness are unable to feel **compassion** for others, which can lead to acts of crime. Mental-health problems such as depression, anxiety, and poor anger management are also **factors**. Reducing crime simply means improving mental health, believe psychologists.

[2] Sociologists, meanwhile, place the blame for crime on social problems. Poverty, unemployment, income inequality, and **discrimination**, they say, are all common causes of crime. For cities everywhere, reducing and preventing crime is a major goal. Sociologists believe that there is just one effective way to do this: Fix society's ills. As society becomes fairer and more inclusive, the crime rate will automatically drop.

[3] Recently, a team of criminologists (scientists who study criminal behavior using both psychological and sociological **insights**) carried out a long-term study. They analyzed census data and police records from 301 U.S. cities with populations of over 100,000. One finding is somewhat surprising: Increasing and **maintaining** green spaces like parks and gardens actually lowers a city's crime rate. This refers to property crimes—robbery, arson, and vandalism (damage done to public places on purpose)—as well as violent crimes like mugging, murder, and rape.

[4] Overall, the research found that the most common causes of crime in every city are poverty and inequality. This conclusion backs up the findings of similar past studies. But the criminologists' research found something new. It shows that green space can help lower crime risk, even—or especially—in disadvantaged areas. The link between "urban nature" and reduced property crime risk was found in 300 of the cities studied. The link between green spaces and reduced violent crime was found in all but three cities.

[5] How exactly this works is unclear. One researcher offered this explanation: "Extreme aggression, anger, and stress often predict a person's future criminal behavior. Green space seems to help people **suppress** these feelings." Based on his team's findings, the researcher concluded, "Cities need first and foremost to improve the quality of life for all residents. But to do this, they must also **consider** the design and location of green space."

Notes psychopathy：精神病 / depression：鬱 / carry out：実行する / census data：統計調査（国勢調査）データ / somewhat：いくらか / property crime：財産犯（所有権その他の財産的法益を侵害する犯罪の総称）/ arson：放火 / vandalism：破壊行為 / mugging：強盗 / disadvantaged：不利な条件におかれた / aggression：攻撃性 / predict：予測する / first and foremost：真っ先に / resident：住民

Part 2 Comprehension:
Follow the instructions for each activity below.

A *Choose the correct answer.*

1. Where does criminal behavior come from, according to psychologists?
   a. family background b. character c. schooling
2. Which of these feelings do people who suffer from psychopathy NOT feel?
   a. anger b. depression c. sympathy for others
3. Which of the following is NOT mentioned as a social problem that can lead to criminal acts?
   a. inequality b. unemployment c. social media

B *Circle T if the sentence is true, F if it is false.*

4. T F Sociologists tend to believe that as society "fixes" its ills or problems, the crime rate will go down.
5. T F The criminologists' study took only a short time to complete.
6. T F A city with a population of one million people would NOT be included in the study.
7. T F Throwing rocks at windows in a public building is an example of the property crime known as vandalism.

C *Match these sentence beginnings with the sentence endings below. Write the letters of the sentence endings on the lines. One ending will not be used. Listen to check your answers.*

DL 18

8. Poverty and social inequality ... ______
9. Disadvantaged areas ... ______
10. In all the cities in the research, a lower risk of crime ... ______

a. are the parts of a city where there is much poverty.
b. was linked to nature and green spaces.
c. have no effect on criminal behavior.
d. lead to more crimes than any other factors or social problems.

D ***Writing Challenge:*** *Write a full-sentence answer to each question below. Listen to check your answers.*

DL 19

11. What most likely is meant by the underlined word "inclusive" as it is used in paragraph 2?

____

12. According to one researcher, how might cities use the findings of the recent research study to "improve the quality of life for all residents"?

____

Part 3 Vocabulary Study: Follow the instructions for each activity below.

A *Match these KEY WORDS from today's reading with the definitions and synonyms below. Write the words on the lines. (The words are highlighted in bold in the reading.)*

compassion	consider	discrimination	factor
insight	maintain	suppress	urban

1. ____________________ to think about seriously; take into account
2. ____________________ having to do with large cities; metropolitan
3. ____________________ to keep up; take good care of; keep in good condition
4. ____________________ feeling pity for the pain or troubles of other people
5. ____________________ a cause or condition; influence; circumstance
6. ____________________ to keep from happening; prevent from occurring; push down
7. ____________________ a good idea; perception; vision; understanding
8. ____________________ unfair treatment of certain people; prejudice; intolerance

B *Match the idiomatic phrases or phrasal verbs on the left with their meanings and synonyms on the right. Write the letters on the lines.*

1. ______ back up	a. especially; specifically
2. ______ first and foremost	b. deliberately; intentionally
3. ______ in particular	c. support; prove; bear out
4. ______ lead to	d. most importantly; before everything else
5. ______ on purpose	e. cause; bring about

Part 4 Listening Challenge: Listen to the short talk. Then fill in the blank in each sentence-definition below with one of these key words and phrases that are used in the talk. Listen to check your answers.

DL 20

abused	crowd control	law-abiding citizens	law enforcement
search-and-rescue	surveillance	thermal cameras	

1. Large events like outdoor rock concerts use drones for ____________________.
2. Drones equipped with ____________________ can detect heat.
3. ____________________ are people who have NOT committed a crime.
4. ____________________ is another way to say "police."
5. A drone that is ____________________ is used for a bad purpose.
6. Drones that do ____________________ keep watch on suspicious people.
7. Lost hikers can be found by using ____________________ drones.

Lesson 5

Everyday Science and Technology (1)

Discoveries and Inventions

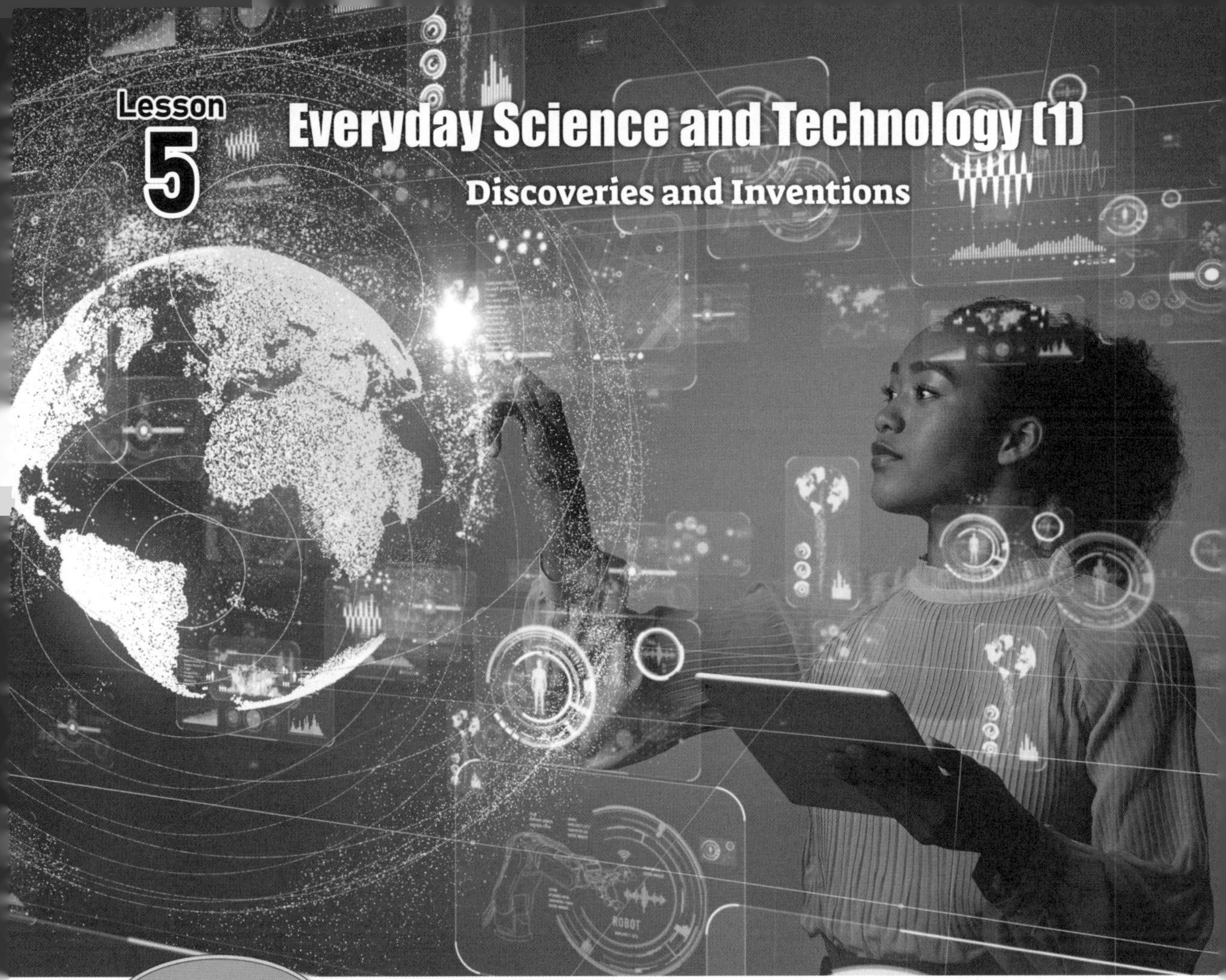

Looking Ahead

As you read today's reading on the next page, look for answers to these questions.

1. What does JWST stand for?
2. What kind of orbit is JWST in?
3. When did JWST begin sending back images from deep space?
4. How long did it take a test "mini-brain" to learn to play Pong?
5. How does a disease called dementia affect the brain?
6. What is meant by plastic's "durability"? In what way is durability bad for the environment?
7. How is a certain caterpillar's saliva helping to solve the plastic recycling problem?

Part 1 Reading:

Read the essay below and do the activities that follow.

DL 21

Introduction: Exciting new discoveries and inventions are being made in every field of science and technology all the time—every day, in fact. Here are three of the latest and, I hope, the most useful to you.

[1] On Christmas Day, 2021, space agencies from the United States, Canada, and Europe **collaborated** to launch the ten-billion-dollar James Webb Space Telescope (JWST). It is the largest, most powerful space telescope ever built. On January 8, 2022, the telescope's **enormous** mirror, measuring seven meters across, was **deployed**, making JWST ready to carry out its scientific operations. On January 24, 2022, the mission team put the telescope into orbit around the Sun, approximately one million miles from Earth. In July 2022, JWST sent back to Earth its first spectacular, high-resolution images—pictures of far-flung ancient galaxies as they were 13 billion years ago. "The observatory is taking us back to the Big Bang. It is giving us a **glimpse** of how the universe began," said a proud and excited NASA astronomer.

[2] In October 2022, Australian researchers used stem cells and mouse embryos to grow a "sentient" mini-brain in a laboratory. Incredibly, they then connected the mini-brain to the **vintage** video game Pong. It took the mini-brain a surprisingly short time—just five minutes—to learn to play the game, says one neuroscientist: "Our mini-brain can take in information from an **external** source, **process** it, and then respond to it." What is the point of such an experiment? "Hopefully, our research will one day aid in the treatment of brain diseases like dementia that damage memory," the researcher added. Obviously, he explained, the brain has no consciousness. "It didn't know it was playing a game, as a human would."

[3] Plastic is designed to last a long, long time. But the **synthetic** product's durability causes a major problem in the environment: mountains of plastic waste. Plastic very slowly breaks down into minuscule specks or molecules. These tiny molecules pollute the earth's water, get into seafood, and end up in humans' lungs and blood. The world's recycling system is struggling to deal with all this harmful plastic waste. But a recent "accidental" discovery may help. Researchers have found that the saliva—the spit—of a certain kind of caterpillar (the larval stage of the wax moth) can quickly cause plastic to degrade. Eventually, this discovery could be used to get rid of plastic at waste-management plants. It may even make at-home plastic-degrading kits possible.

Notes agency：～庁、局 / James Webb Space Telescope (JWST)：ジェイムズ・ウェッブ宇宙望遠鏡（アメリカ航空宇宙局（NASA）が中心となって開発された赤外線観測用宇宙望遠鏡）/ measure：～の長さ［幅、高さ、量］がある / across：直径 / orbit：軌道 / high-revolution：高解像度の / far-flung：広範囲にわたる、遠く離れた / observatory：観測用人工衛星 / stem cell：幹細胞（分化した細胞のもととなる細胞）/ mouse embryo：マウス胚（胚とは受胎後間もない生体のこと）/ laboratory：実験室 / neuroscientist：神経科学者 / experiment：実験 / dementia：認知症 / miniscule：極めて小さい / speck：小さな粒 / molecule：微片、微分子 / saliva：唾液 / spit：つば / larval：幼虫の、幼生の / wax moth：ハチミツガ / degrade：分解する / waste-management plant：ごみ処理工場

Part 2 Comprehension:
Follow the instructions for each activity below.

A *Today's reading deals with three fields of science. Match each lettered scientific field on the right with the number on the left of the paragraph in today's reading that the scientific field refers to. Write the letters on the lines.*

1. [1] _____ a. neuroscience [study of the brain and nerves]
2. [2] _____ b. microbiology [study of very small organisms]
3. [3] _____ c. astrophysics [study of objects and events in space]

B *Choose the correct answer.*

4. How much did JWST cost to build?
   a. $1,000,0000 b. $10,000,000 c. $10,000,000,000
5. How far is JWST from Earth?
   a. 1,000,000 miles b. 1,000,000 kilometers c. 100,000 kilometers

C *Circle T if the sentence is true, F if it is false.*

6. T F The underlined word "sentient" as used in paragraph 2 most likely means "able to feel or perceive things."
7. T F The mini-brain grown in a laboratory knew that it was playing a game.
8. T F The big problem with plastic is that it lasts such a long time once it gets into the environment.
9. T F So far, no dangerous plastic "specks" have been found in humans.

D ***Writing Challenge:*** *Write a full-sentence answer to each question below. Listen to check your answers.* DL 22

10. What might we be able to learn thanks to the James Webb Space Telescope's operations and images?

____

11. What practical use might come out of the "mini-brain" that was recently created in a laboratory in Australia?

____

12. How might the accidental discovery about a certain caterpillar's saliva help us reduce plastic waste?

____

Part 3 Vocabulary Study: Follow the instructions for each activity below.

A *Fill in the blank in each sentence-definition or description below with one of these words. (The words are highlighted in bold in the reading.)*

collaborate	deploy	enormous	external
glimpse	process	synthetic	vintage

1. A ______________ diamond isn't the real thing; it was made by people.
2. When you get just a ______________ of the moon, you get a very brief look at it.
3. The verb ______________ is a formal way to say "put to use somewhere."
4. You get better results if you ______________, that is, work together with someone.
5. The walls inside a house are internal; those on the outside are ______________.
6. If you pay an ______________ amount of money for a new car, you pay a very high price for it.
7. As a noun, ______________ refers to a step-by-step way of doing something, but as a verb, it means to work on something in order to change or preserve it.
8. If you're looking for a ______________ dress or suit from the 1950s or 1960s, say, the best place to go is to a recycled clothing store.

B *Complete each sentence below with one of these sentence-beginning adverbs from today's reading. Write the adverbs on the lines. Listen to check your answers.*

Eventually	Hopefully	Incredibly	Obviously

DL 23

1. Right now, painting is my hobby. ______________, though, I would like to display and sell my works in a gallery.
2. This isn't a real Rolex. Look at this cheap material! ______________, the watch is a fake.
3. Bill speaks perfect Chinese. ______________, however, he has never been to Taiwan or China.
4. This novel I'm reading now is really dark and depressing. ______________, however, it will have a happy ending.

Part 4 Listening Challenge: Listen to the sentences, all of which are based on today's reading. Circle T if the sentence you hear is true, or F if it is false.

DL 24

1. T F **2.** T F **3.** T F **4.** T F

Lesson 6

Ecology/Environmental Science (2)

Cop15: Biodiversity

Looking Ahead

As you read today's reading on the next page, look for answers to these questions.

1. Who attended a biodiversity conference that was recently held in Montreal, Canada?
2. What made the conference unique?
3. What did the agreement that was reached at the conference pledge to do about biodiversity?
4. What percentages of Earth's land and water are now protected?
5. In what ways do humans rely on biodiversity?
6. What does one dark, pessimistic report have to say about plant and animal extinction?
7. Who is Inger Andersen, and what does she say we have to change?

Part 1 Reading:
Read the essay below and do the activities that follow. DL 25

[1] On December 7, 2022, the U.N. Biodiversity Conference convened in Montreal, Canada. Some 15,000 government and business leaders, scientists, and indigenous peoples from around the globe were in attendance. Their objective was to protect biodiversity—all the living plant and animal species that exist on our planet. The **summit**, dubbed Cop15, was unique: For the first time, many children and teenagers sat in on panels and seminars and had a chance to voice their insights and hopes for a greener future.

[2] Representatives from 190 nations had the task of hammering out a deal to halt humans' **devastation** of nature. On December 19, after two weeks of **contentious** negotiation, an agreement was reached. It pledged to protect 30 percent of Earth's terrestrial areas and 30 percent of its marine areas by 2030. Currently, only 17 percent of land and ten percent of oceans have been set aside for protection.

[3] What makes protecting biodiversity so important? Without a wide variety of plants, animals, and microorganisms, we humans would not have the healthy ecosystems we depend on. Biodiversity provides us with the air we breathe, the food we eat, and the medicines we use to ward off and cure illness.

[4] But for centuries, humans have been assaulting nature. We have been **greedily** taking from it without giving much back. Climate change and the loss of habitats stemming from land and ocean development have been robbing Earth of its biodiversity. One **pessimistic** report predicts that over the next few decades, more than one million plant and animal species will become extinct. Preventing this tragedy is why **implementing** Cop15's ambitious goals is so **imperative**. Most attendees were optimistic that these **objectives** can be achieved. But others, judging from past failures to meet previously set goals, are doubtful. They are worried that actions will fall short of words.

[5] Inger Andersen, the U.N.'s environment chief, is one of the hopeful attendees. "We need to change the relationship between people and nature," she told the press after the conference. "If we are honest, time is not on our side. We've backed nature into a corner. But nature is remarkable and very forgiving. If we give it half a chance—which is what Cop15 does—nature will bounce back."

Notes the U.N. Biodiversity Conference：国連生物多様性条約会議（生物多様性条約を締約した国が生物多様性その他の問題について話し合うために定期的に開催している会議）/ convene：開催される / dub：～と称する / green：環境に配慮した、環境に優しい / representative：代表、使節 / hammer out：～を努力を重ねてつくり上げる / deal：協定、取決め / halt：中止、停止させる / pledge：誓約する、確約する / terrestrial：陸上の / microorganism：微生物 / ward off：～を防ぐ / assault：襲撃、攻撃する / habitat：生物の生息地 / stem from：～に由来する / extinct：死に絶えた、絶滅した / attendee：出席者 / fall short of：～に達しない、及ばない、届かない / forgiving：寛大な / bounce back = recover：回復する

Part 2 Comprehension:
Follow the instructions for each activity below.

A *Choose the correct answer.*

1. It can be inferred from the context that the underlined word "indigenous"
   a. is a synonym for "biodiversity." b. refers to native peoples.
   c. is a kind of scientist who specializes in biodiversity.
2. At the conference, for the first time, young people were able to
   a. add their opinions to discussions.
   b. get autographs from other conference attendees.
   c. take courses to learn all about biodiversity.
3. The goal of the attendees to the conference was to
   a. conduct research on living species.
   b. preserve and protect the living species that still remain on our planet.
   c. determine the exact number of different living species on Earth.

B *Circle T if the sentence is true, F if it is false.*

4. T F All 15,000 Cop15 attendees in Montreal negotiated the new deal.
5. T F The agreement was fairly easy to negotiate.
6. T F The goals "hammered out" in the deal are set to be realized by 2030.

C *Fill in the numbered blanks in the short paragraph below.*
Listen to check your answers. DL 26

Without biodiversity, Earth's ecosystems would not be (7)______________. But humans have been taking too much from nature without giving enough back. Climate change and (8)______________ have been destroying the habitats in which biodiversity exists. One report says that more than a million plant and animal species will become extinct over the next few (9)______________. The Cop15 conference took some steps to try to prevent this (10)______________.

D ***Writing Challenge:*** *Write a full-sentence answer to each question below.*
Listen to check your answers. DL 27

11. What are some things that biodiversity provides that enable us to survive?

____

12. What most likely does Inger Andersen, the U.N.'s chief environmentalist, mean when she says, "If we are honest, time is not on our side"?

____

Part 3 Vocabulary Study: *Follow the instructions for each activity below.*

A *Match these KEY WORDS from today's reading with the definitions and synonyms below. Write the words on the lines. (The words are highlighted in bold in the reading.)*

contentious	devastation	greedily	imperative
implement	objective	pessimistic	summit

1. ____________________ a. a goal or aim; target; intention
2. ____________________ b. very important; absolutely necessary; essential
3. ____________________ c. a high-level conference
4. ____________________ d. causing debate or argument
5. ____________________ e. to put into action, effect, or practice; realize
6. ____________________ f. widespread destruction; complete or total ruin
7. ____________________ g. expecting the worst to happen; gloomy; cynical
8. ____________________ h. in a way that demands, takes, or uses too much

B *Fill in the blank in each sentence below with the correct form of one of these words to make an idiomatic phrase used in today's reading. Listen to check your answers. (The meaning of the phrase is shown in brackets after each sentence.)*

DL 28

fall	set	stem	ward

1. This new bug spray effectively __________ **off** mosquitoes. [keep away]
2. Once again, the swimmer has __________ **short of** the world record. [fail to reach]
3. Have you been __________ **aside** money for university? [save; put away]
4. Dick's troubles with his co-workers __________ **from** his bad temper. [caused by]

Part 4 Listening Challenge: General Knowledge Quiz: *Listen to the short descriptions of the six main categories of animals. After you listen to each description, complete each sentence below with one of these animal categories.*

DL 29

amphibians	birds	fish	invertebrates	mammals	reptiles

1. The animals being described are ____________________.
2. The animals being described are ____________________.
3. The animals being described are ____________________.
4. The animals being described are ____________________.
5. The animals being described are ____________________.
6. The animals being described are ____________________.

Lesson 7

Biology/Botany/Mycology

Plant Communication: Is It Real?

Looking Ahead

As you read today's reading on the next page, look for answers to these questions.

1. What does Peter Wohlleben do for a living? What is the name of his book?
2. What controversial claim did he make in his book?
3. What are fungi and how do they become "pipes" and "wires"?
4. What is "photosynthesis"?
5. What is meant by "nutrients"?
6. Who are Andrew Adamatsky and Suzanne Simard? What do they think of the idea that plants can communicate?
7. What does Lincoln Tiaz think of the "wood-wide web" concept?

Part 1 Reading:
Read the essay below and do the activities that follow. DL 30

[1] Do plants talk to one another? Can plants hear us when we talk to them? Are plants intelligent? These **intriguing** questions are hotly debated among scientists in many fields. The answers depend on whom you talk to.

[2] In 2015, a German forester named Peter Wohlleben published a book entitled *The Hidden Life of Trees*. All the trees in a forest, he wrote, are linked through **elaborate** underground networks. This “wood-wide web” is made up of tiny fungi (mushroom-like plants) that line the trees’ roots. The trees and fungi are “partners” that take advantage of and look out for each other. But Wohlleben also made a highly controversial claim: Trees use this network to “talk to” one another.

[3] Wohlleben’s symbiotic arrangement between trees and fungi works like this. The fungi are underground “pipes” through which trees transport water and **vital** nutrients (food) to one another. But the trees also use the fungi to communicate. In this role, fungi become “wires” over which trees send signals that **warn** other trees about drought, disease, insect attacks, and other dangers. When they receive these signals, the other trees alter their behavior to protect themselves. The fungi, meanwhile, benefit, too. Through photosynthesis, trees **convert** sunlight into sugar. The fungi feed on this sugar, giving them the energy they need to take phosphorus, nitrogen, and other minerals out of the soil—the very nutrients that their partner trees cannot live without.

[4] British computer scientist Andrew Adamatsky believes that fungi “talk” using electrical signals. He claims that some species have a vocabulary of 50 words! Suzanne Simard would no doubt back up Adamatsky’s claim. She’s a Canadian forest ecologist who compares the “wood-wide web” to the human brain’s neural networks.

[5] But not all scientists see eye to eye with this “talking plants” idea. For one thing, it lacks **sufficient** supporting scientific evidence, some argue. Lincoln Taiz, a California biologist, thinks the very idea is, to put it bluntly, nonsense. The belief that trees think, feel, and even speak is a **myth**—an example of “anthropomorphism,” Taiz wrote in the journal *Trends in Plant Science*. It shows humans’ **sentimental** need to believe that non-humans act and behave like humans. To Taiz, “intelligent trees” and “conscious plants” are irrational, silly ideas, and nothing more than “wishful thinking.”

Notes forester：森林監督者 / fungi：fungus（菌類、キノコ）の複数形 / line：～に沿って並ぶ / look out for：～の世話をする、面倒を見る / controversial：議論の的になる、議論を呼ぶ / symbiotic：共生の、共生している / arrangement：協定、取決め、取りはからい / nutrient：養分、栄養素 / benefit：利益を得る / photosynthesis：光合成 / phosphorus：（非金属元素の）リン / nitrogen：窒素 / mineral：無機物 / claim：主張、主張する / no doubt：きっと［疑いなく］～だろう / neural：神経の / see eye to eye with：～と意見が合う、見解が一致する / for one thing：一つには / the very：まさしくその / to put it bluntly：遠慮なく言うと / anthropomorphism：擬人化 / wishful：願望に基づいた

Part 2 Comprehension:

Follow the instructions for each activity below.

A *Complete each sentence below.*

1. What does Peter Wohlleben do for a living?

   He's ______________________________.

2. What is the title of his book?

   It is entitled ______________________________.

3. What does he call the underground network of fungi?

   He calls it the "______________________________."

B *Circle T if the sentence is true, F if it is false.*

4. T F Fungi grow on a tree's trunk and limbs.
5. T F All scientists accept Wohlleben's idea that trees "talk."
6. T F The underground fungi work like hammers and screwdrivers.
7. T F "Photosynthesis" is a process whereby trees change sunlight into a kind of food.

C *Fill in the numbered blanks in the short paragraph below.*
Listen to check your answers. DL 31

British computer scientist Andrew Adamatsky believes that forest fungi "talk" using **(8)**________________. He claims that some species have a vocabulary of 50 words! Suzanne Simard would no doubt back up Adamatsky's claim. She's a Canadian **(9)**________________ who compares the "wood-wide web" to the human brain's **(10)**________________.

D ***Writing Challenge:*** *Write a full-sentence answer to each question below.*
Listen to check your answers. DL 32

11. What do some scientists say is the main reason that they cannot accept the idea that trees are intelligent and talk to one another?

    ____

    ____

12. What is meant by the word "anthropomorphism"?

    ____

    ____

Part 3 Vocabulary Study: Follow the instructions for each activity below.

A *Fill in the blank in each sentence-definition or description below with one of these words. (The words are highlighted in bold in the reading.)*

convert	elaborate	intriguing	myth
sentimental	sufficient	vital	warn

1. A ____________ is an ancient story or a false idea that many people think true.
2. When you ____________ people, you tell them to watch out for possible danger.
3. A ____________ idea is one that is based on feeling, not on reason or logic.
4. A chart will help you ____________ or change Fahrenheit to Centigrade.
5. An ____________ novel, say, is one that is very interesting and perhaps mysterious.
6. Good synonyms for ____________ include essential, imperative, and critical.
7. If you have ____________ money for your rent and other monthly expenses, you have enough money.
8. "This drawing is very ____________. It has so many details," said one art lover.

B *Match the idiomatic phrases or phrasal verbs on the left with their meanings and synonyms on the right. Write the letters on the lines.*

1. _____	be made up of	a. use as food; eat
2. _____	feed on	b. agree; comply
3. _____	look out for	c. consist of; have as parts
4. _____	no doubt	d. take care of; protect; defend
5. _____	see eye to eye	e. surely; of course

Part 4 Listening Challenge: As you listen to the short talk, fill in each blank below. Listen again to check your answers.

DL 33

"Symbiosis" is a natural ____________ where two different plant or animal ____________ depend on each other. One example of symbiosis is that between a goby fish and a shrimp. The shrimp digs a hole in the sea floor's sand for itself and its goby fish ____________ to live in. The fish keeps this ____________ "house" clean. But the goby does more than that. Because the shrimp is nearly ____________, it is at risk of ____________ from predators such as sharks or other fish that want to feed on it. When the goby fish sees a predator coming, it ____________ its partner shrimp by touching it with its ____________. The goby fish and the shrimp then ____________ into their shared "house," out of ____________.

Lesson 8

Robotics

Human-Machine Interaction

Looking Ahead

As you read today's reading on the next page, look for answers to these questions.

1. What is the "uncanny valley"?
2. What are "humanoid robots"? Where are they being used more and more these days?
3. What is meant by the phrase "employee-turnover rate"?
4. Who recently conducted a psychological research survey on robot-human interactions?
5. What were the people who participated in the survey asked to describe?
6. Which gender of robot did the respondents in the survey prefer?
7. What did Soobin Seo conclude about the results of the research study?

Part 1 Reading:
Read the essay below and do the activities that follow. DL 34

[1] Perhaps you've heard of the "uncanny valley." This is a term in psychology that describes the unease or even **disgust** people feel when they are confronted with avatars, androids, and animated characters—but especially with humanoid robots—that look extremely life-like. There is now a wealth of research data, however, that shows that as humanoid robots have grown more common in industrial, business, and service applications, people are becoming more used to them. They now see them as more **empathetic** and trustworthy than completely "inhuman" machines.

[2] One place where interactions between people and robots are increasingly frequent is in the hospitality industry. Even prior to the COVID-19 pandemic, hotels, restaurants, and other venues were struggling with a high employee-turnover rate. That's why so many are now resorting to robots to perform various functions. This trend **prompted** researchers at Washington State University to conduct an interesting study. The research aimed to **ascertain** if **typical** psychological relationships seen in human-to-human interactions also hold true in human-to-robot interactions.

[3] To carry out the study, psychologists surveyed 170 people on their reactions to four different **hypothetical** service-robot scenarios. In one scenario, survey respondents were greeted by a male robot named "Alex," who had a human face and human-like body. A second scenario had the same script, except for two differences: The robot's gender was female and its name was "Sara." In two other scenarios, the robots were female and male, respectively, but they were very "machine-like" with an interactive screen in place of a face. The respondents were then asked to describe how they felt about each scenario. According to sciencedaily.com, "The participants who saw the female-robot scenarios **rated** the experience as more pleasant and satisfying than those who had scenarios with male robots. Also, the preference for the female robot was stronger the more humanoid the robot was."

[4] Professor Soobin Seo, who led the study, summed up her team's findings like this: "People tend to feel more comfortable being cared for by females because of existing gender ideas about service roles. That **stereotype** appears to transfer to robot interactions and becomes more obvious the more human-like the robots are."

Notes uncanny：薄気味悪い / are confronted with：～に直面する / humanoid：人間の形をした、人間に似た / life-like：生きているような / application：応用、実地に適用できること / hospitality：親切なもてなし、歓待、接待 / prior to：～より前に / COVID-19：新型コロナウィルス感染症 / pandemic：流行性の、流行病 / venue：会場、開催地 / struggle：もがく、あがく、苦闘する / turnover rate：離職率 / resort to：～に助けを求める / conduct：実施する / hold true：当てはまる / carry out：実施する / scenario：シナリオ、筋書 / script：脚本、台本 / except for：～を除いて、～のほかは / respectively：それぞれ / in place of：～の代わりに / humanoid：人間そっくりの / sum up：要約する / existing：既存の / transfer to：～に移動する、移転する

Part 2 Comprehension:
Follow the instructions for each activity below.

A *Choose the correct answer.*

1. In the "uncanny valley," what do people feel when they come face to face with a humanoid robot?
   a. at ease b. unease c. easier
2. Which of the following is NOT mentioned as an application where robots are more frequently being put to use these days?
   a. industry and business b. the service industries c. entertainment and sports
3. What has changed about the way people see humanoid robots these days?
   a. They trust them more. b. They prefer them to humans.
   c. They are still always upset by them.

B *Circle T if the sentence is true, F if it is false.*

4. T F The phrase "hospitality industry" refers to medical care.
5. T F Hotels' and restaurants' problems with hiring and keeping employees began because of the COVID-19 pandemic.
6. T F Researchers at Washington State University hoped to learn if human-to-robot interactions were in any way similar to human-to-human interactions.

C *Fill in the blanks in the sentences below with a word or phrase from the reading. Listen to check your answers.* DL 35

7. In the first two research-study scenarios, the male and female robots were named Alex and Sara, ________________.
8. In the other two scenarios, the two robots were male and female but had different names and an ________________ ________________ for a face.
9. The research ________________ asked the ________________ to describe how they felt during each scenario.
10. The people who met the female robots felt more ________________ with them, especially when the robot was more ________________.

D ***Writing Challenge:*** *Write a full-sentence answer to each question below. Listen to check your answers.* DL 36

11. How have hotels and restaurants dealt with the high employee-turnover rate?

____

12. What would you say is the main idea expressed in today's reading?

____

Part 3 Vocabulary Study: Follow the instructions for each activity below.

A *Match these KEY WORDS from today's reading with their definitions and synonyms below. Write the words on the lines. (The words are highlighted in bold in the reading.)*

ascertain	disgust	empathetic	hypothetical
prompt	rate	stereotype	typical

1. ________________ a strong feeling that something is very unpleasant
2. ________________ to inspire or cause someone to do something
3. ________________ based on a situation that is imagined, made up, or not true
4. ________________ to find something out for sure or certain; learn
5. ________________ to give something a numbered value, such as 1 to 10
6. ________________ feeling sympathy for others' conditions or problems
7. ________________ characteristic; usual; normal
8. ________________ a very simple, often biased idea of a person or thing; cliché

B *Fill in the blank in each sentence below with the correct form of one of these words to complete a common phrase. Listen to check your answers.*

DL 37

aim	prior	resort	tend

1. To prevent injury, make sure you warm up ____________ **to** working out.
2. People ____________ **to** be hurt when you mention their weight or appearance.
3. The new online course ____________ **to** give people more self-confidence.
4. The student hadn't studied for the test, so he ____________ **to** cheating.

Part 4 Listening Challenge: Listen to the short talk and then write a brief answer to each question below. Listen to check your answers.

DL 38

1. What kind of movie is *M3GAN*?

   ____

2. What or who is M3GAN?

   ____

3. What has M3GAN been programmed to do?

   ____

4. What human trait does M3GAN develop?

   ____

5. What does jealousy make M3GAN become?

   ____

6. Where, according to one critic, should we see a movie like *M3GAN*?

   ____

Lesson 9

Solar Power/Nanotechnology

A Promising Energy Future

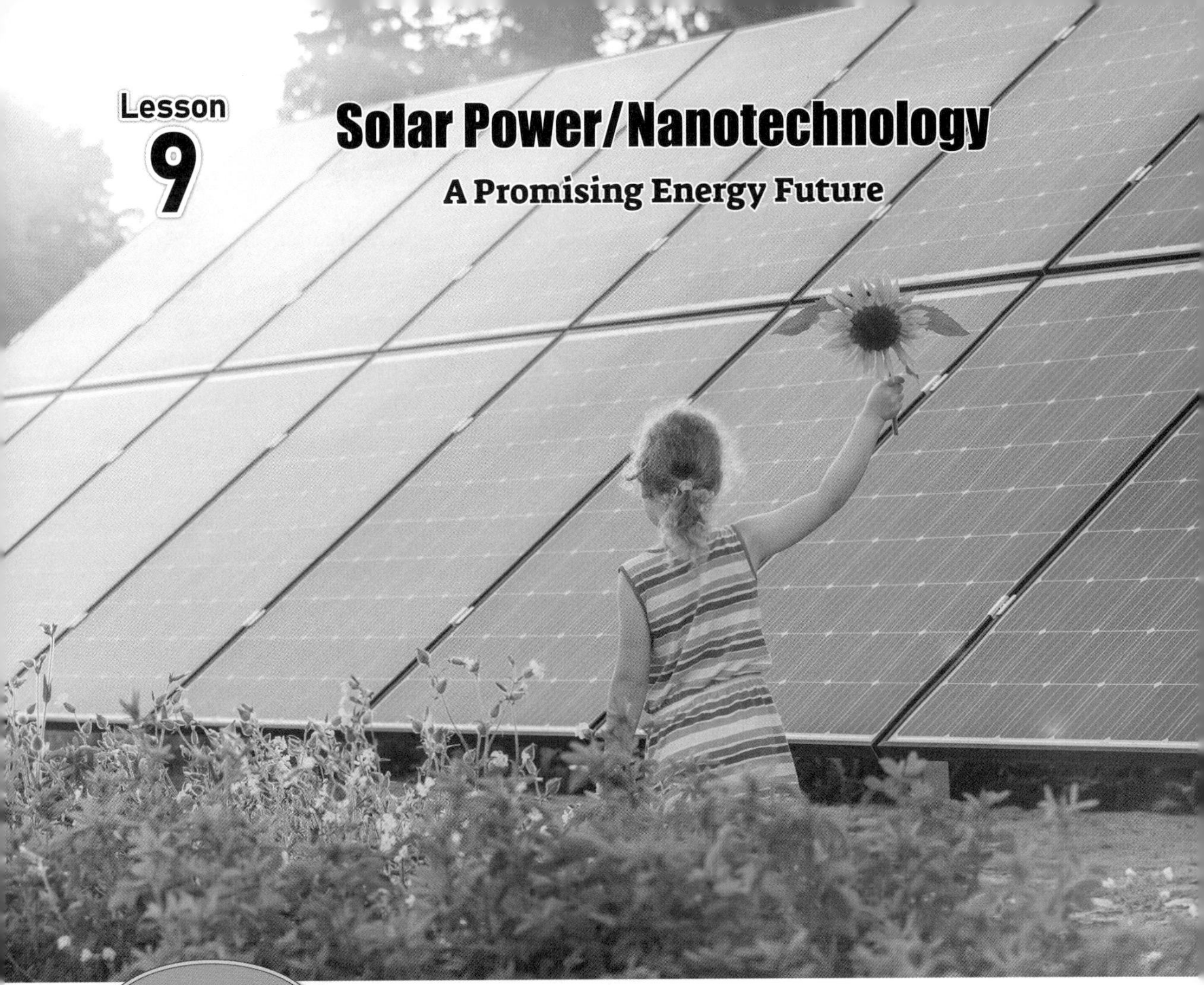

Looking Ahead

As you read today's reading on the next page, look for answers to these questions.

1. In 2022, how much of the world's energy came from solar power?
2. What are two reasons why solar power is NOT used as much as it should or could be?
3. In 2017, what happened at Sweden's Chalmers University?
4. How about in 2022?
5. Why is the Chalmers development team so optimistic?
6. How might we use the new solar batteries made possible by an MIT invention?
7. What does one MIT engineer call the MIT invention?

Part 1 Reading:

Read the essay below and do the activities that follow.

DL 39

[1] Solar power represents mankind's best hope for a brighter, greener, cleaner future. But in 2022, only five percent of the world's total energy came from solar power. There are two **salient** reasons for this. To **capture** and use solar power is expensive. Solar power is also inefficient, primarily because of problems related to storing and transporting the energy produced. But thanks to research-and-development efforts to overcome these **shortcomings**, even 2022's "meager solar usage," as a Harvard researcher put it, "is a major improvement over what it was two decades ago."

[2] Two remarkable recent technological advances promise to make solar power a far less costly and far more useful energy source. The first breakthrough came in 2017 from a team of engineers at Chalmers University of Technology in Sweden. They invented a system that can capture solar energy and **store** it not just for today's four or five days, but for up to 18 years!

[3] Then, in 2022, the same team, in collaboration with engineers at Shanghai Jiao Tong University, made another breakthrough. They developed solar batteries that allow electronic devices like smartwatches and headphones to constantly self-charge. The batteries do this no matter what the weather, time of day, season, or location. Admittedly, the **innovative** technology is still limited to smaller solar batteries. But these promising results have increased optimism in the scientific community. It is now speculated that the method will one day replace solar batteries and solar cells altogether and lead to applications on larger and larger scales.

[4] Likewise for a breakthrough made last year at the Massachusetts Institute of Technology (MIT). There, nanotechnology engineers have developed **durable**, flexible, ultralight, paper-thin solar cells that can be **adhered** onto all kinds of surfaces. The new cells, says MIT, can provide energy as a wearable fabric or be rapidly deployed to remote locations. For example, they might be stuck onto tents and tarps in rescue operations at disaster sites. They could also be stuck onto the wings of drones to **extend** flying range or onto the sails of yachts to provide power at sea.

[5] More research is required to give the new cells more applications. But MIT's development team leader is optimistic. He believes that this breakthrough gives us "a unique opportunity to rethink what solar technology looks like and how we deploy it."

Notes green：環境保護主義の / research and development：研究開発 / meager：乏しい、不十分な / improvement over：～と比べて改善されたもの / breakthrough：大きな進歩、躍進 / Chalmers University of Technology：（スウェーデンの）チャルマース工科大学 / today's：今の、現時点での / Shanghai Jiao Tong University：上海交通大学 / battery：充電池 / self-charge：自己充電する / admittedly：確かに、疑いもなく / optimism：楽観主義 / speculate：推測する / replace：～に取って代わる / altogether：完全に / likewise for：～も同様である / Massachusetts Institute of Technology（MIT）：マサチューセッツ工科大学 / nanotechnology：ナノテクノロジー（物質を非常に小さいスケールにおいて自在に制御する技術のこと）/ ultralight：超軽量の / surface：表面 / fabric：織物、生地 / deploy：展開する、配置する / stuck：stick（固着させる）の過去分詞形 / tarp：防水シート / disaster：災害 / flying range：飛行距離 / sail：帆

Part 2 Comprehension:
Follow the instructions for each activity below.

A *Listen to the "OR" questions. Write a short, full-sentence answer to each question on the lines below. Listen to check your answers.*

DL 40

1. ______________________________

2. ______________________________

3. ______________________________

4. ______________________________

B *Circle T if the sentence is true, F if it is false.*

5. T F Solar power is relatively easy to store and transport.
6. T F Thanks to research in Sweden, solar power can now be stored for five or six days.
7. T F The Chalmers University-Shanghai Jiao Tong University scientists are optimistic about the future of their invention.

C *Fill in the blanks in the sentences below.*

8. MIT's newly developed solar cells can be used in ______________ locations such as ______________ sites.
9. To provide energy, they can be stuck onto various ______________, including the ______________ of yachts.
10. The MIT development team leader calls the ______________ a unique ______________.

D ***Writing Challenge:*** *Write a full-sentence answer to each question below. Listen to check your answers.*

DL 41

11. Why does one Harvard researcher call 2022's total solar-power usage "meager"?

____

____

12. As far as their future applications are concerned, what do the two engineering breakthroughs discussed in today's reading have in common?

____

____

Part 3 Vocabulary Study: Follow the instructions for each activity below.

A *Fill in the blank in each sentence-definition or description below with one of these words. (The words are highlighted in bold in the reading.)*

adhere	capture	durable	extend
innovative	salient	shortcoming	store

1. The more ______________ a pair of jeans are, the longer they last.
2. If your essay has a ______________, there is something wrong with it.
3. An ______________ idea is one that is new and creative.
4. You can stick or ______________ Post-its onto the pages of books.
5. To ______________ or lengthen the traveling distance of your e-bicycle battery, you have to recharge it.
6. A ______________ feature of a new camera is a very important feature of it.
7. These days, people like to rent "trunk rooms" to ______________ or keep their extra furniture and other stuff in.
8. As a kid, I liked to ______________ or catch cicadas and keep them in little cages.

B *Fill in the blank in each sentence below with one of these common phrases used in today's reading. The words or phrases in bold italics are more formal synonyms.*

no matter what	one day	thanks to	up to

1. Instead of saying that something will ***eventually*** happen, you might say that it will happen ________________.
2. The phrase ________________ is another way to say ***regardless of***.
3. We often say ________________ when we mean ***as much as*** OR ***as long as***.
4. The formal phrase ***as a result of*** can be replaced with ________________.

Part 4 Listening Challenge: Dictation: As you listen to the sentences about solar power and energy, write what you hear on the lines below.

DL 42

1. ____.
2. ____.
3. ____.
4. ____.
5. ____.
6. ____.

Lesson 10

Everyday Science and Technology (2)

Progress and Hope

Looking Ahead

As you read today's reading on the next page, look for answers to these questions.

1. These days, what is causing extreme weather events to become more frequent?
2. How are many lives and large amounts of money being saved each year?
3. Who is Antonio Guterres? When did he make a speech about early-warning systems for extreme weather events?
4. What did an experiment conducted recently in a California laboratory accomplish?
5. Who is Jennifer M. Granholm? What did she think of the results of the California "miracle"?
6. How is "base editing" different from standard CRISPR gene editing?
7. Why did one U.K. girl need treatment? How is the treatment working?

Part 1 Reading:
Read the essay below and do the activities that follow.

DL 43

Introduction: Progress is being made in every field of science and technology all the time—every day in fact. This is giving the world hope for a brighter, safer, greener, healthier, and more just future. Here are three recent examples of such progress.

[1] Global warming is making extreme weather and natural-hazard events more frequent—and people more **vulnerable** to them. In this situation, early warnings are our best hope of preventing tragedy. Prior alerts, even of only 24 hours, can cut down on damage and death by up to forty percent. Today, meteorologists' improved ability to **anticipate** cyclones, heatwaves, floods, and droughts is saving innumerable lives and billions of dollars in property each year. But, **lamented** U.N. Secretary General Antonio Guterres on World Meteorological Day 2022, "One third of the world's people, mainly in least-developed countries and small island states, are not covered by such systems." Calling this situation "unacceptable," he pledged to "invest equally in adaptation and **resilience**" and to make early-alert systems truly universal.

[2] Nuclear physicists in a California laboratory made headlines in December 2022 when they announced a miracle of sorts: They had used the world's most powerful laser to demonstrate a nuclear-fusion reaction in which more energy was put out than consumed. "This takes energy-generation out of the realm of science fiction into a possible real-world power source," said one physicist. Though it may take decades to realize fusion's full **potential**, U.S. Energy Secretary Jennifer M. Granholm was elated. "This milestone moves us one step closer to using fusion energy to produce unlimited electricity, clean transportation fuels, power for heavy industry, and so much more," she said.

[3] CRISPR is a pioneering gene-editing technology that scientists use to alter DNA. "Base editing" is an advanced type of CRISPR that allows geneticists to make **precise**, single-letter changes. Although the technique is still in its infancy, "It's stunning to watch how quickly new inventions are moving from the lab into promising cures," said journalist Lisa Jarvis. Take, for example, Alyssa, a 13-year-old U.K. girl who had been **diagnosed** with an **acute** form of leukemia. She recently became the world's first person to be treated with the new technique, which was developed by Dr. Waseem Qasim at University College London. Alyssa's cancer has been "undetectable since she started the treatment." "Alyssa is only one patient, so it's too soon to say 'cure,'" says Lisa Jarvis. "But it's worth celebrating the U.K. success"—and the hope it stands for.

Notes natural-hazard：自然災害の / prior：事前の / cut down on：～を削減する / up to：～まで / meteorologist：気象学者 / heatwave：熱波、酷暑 / innumerable：数え切れぬほどの / property：資産 / U.N. Secretary General：国際連合事務総長 / World Meteorological Day：世界気象デー（1950 年に世界気象機関条約が発効したことを記念して制定された国際デー）/ pledge to：～することを誓う / nuclear physicist：原子物理学者 / laboratory：研究所、実験室 / make headlines：メディアで大きく報道される / of sorts：ある種の、一種の / nuclear-fusion reaction：核融合反応 / put out：生産する、産出する / realm：範囲、領域 / U.S. Energy Secretary：アメリカ合衆国エネルギー長官 / elate：得意がらせる / milestone：（歴史上の）画期的事件 / heavy industry：重工業 / pioneering：先駆的な / base editing：塩基編集（DNA を切断することなく編集すること）/ geneticist：遺伝学者 / in its infancy：初期段階、揺籃期にある / stunning：驚くべき / lab：実験室 / leukemia：白血病 / undetectable：検知できない

Part 2 Comprehension:

Follow the instructions for each activity below.

A *Today's reading deals with three fields of science. Match each lettered scientific field on the right with the number on the left of the paragraph that the scientific or technological field refers to. Write the letters on the lines.*

1. [1] ______ a. genetics and medical science
2. [2] ______ b. nuclear physics
3. [3] ______ c. meteorology and disaster prevention

B *Choose the correct answer.*

4. What are early warnings our best hope for preventing?
   a. climate change b. extreme weather events c. tragedy
5. What percentage of the world's people are not covered by natural-disaster, early-warning systems?
   a. 33% b. 50% c. 67%
6. What did U.N. Secretary General Antonio Guterres recently promise to do?
   a. Give a speech on World Meteorological Day.
   b. Make early warning systems available to everyone.
   c. Stop global warming.

C *Circle T if the sentence is true, F if it is false.*

7. T F In the California laboratory experiment, more energy was produced than consumed.
8. T F Nuclear fusion will very soon be producing unlimited electricity.

D *Fill in the blanks in each sentence below. Listen to check your answers.* DL 44

9. Lisa Jarvis is a ______________ who thinks the ______________ form of CRISPR is worth ______________.
10. Alyssa is a 13-year-old girl in the U.K. who underwent a new leukemia ______________, which was ______________ by Dr. Waseem Qasim.

E ***Writing Challenge:*** *Write a full-sentence answer to each question below. Listen to check your answers.* DL 45

11. What makes the current situation in regard to early warning "unacceptable" to Antonio Guterres?

____

12. Today's paragraphs all have the theme of "hope" in common. What makes them hopeful?

____

Part 3 *Vocabulary Study: Follow the instructions for each activity below.*

A *Match these KEY WORDS from today's reading with their definitions and synonyms below. Write the words on the lines. (The words are highlighted in bold in the reading.)*

acute	anticipate	diagnose	lament
potential	precise	resilience	vulnerable

1. ______________ a. very accurate; exact; specific
2. ______________ b. very serious or bad; severe; dire
3. ______________ c. in danger; at risk; open to attack; in jeopardy
4. ______________ d. to identify or name a disease or illness
5. ______________ e. ability to recover from difficult situations; toughness
6. ______________ f. to predict; see ahead; guess what will happen
7. ______________ g. possible or probable; likely
8. ______________ h. to feel bad or sorry about; regret

B *Answer each question below with one of these idiomatic phrases from today's reading passage. Write the phrases on the lines.*

cut down on	make headlines	put out	stand for

1. Which phrase would you use to talk about reducing the use of plastic?

   ____

2. Which phrase would help you report how many e-bikes a factory produces?

   ____

3. Which phrase would help you explain what the stars in the U.S. flag represent?

   ____

4. Which phrase would you use to write about an amazing new discovery?

   ____

Part 4 ***Listening Challenge:*** *Read the sentences below. Make sure you understand the word in bold in each sentence. Then listen to the short talk and circle T if each sentence below is true, or F if it is false.*

DL 46

1. T F Natural disasters are growing in **intensity** and frequency.
2. T F The new method to **track** disasters uses old technologies.
3. T F Machine learning doesn't **involve** giving machines data or information.
4. T F "Remote sensing" is made possible by **satellites** orbiting Earth.
5. T F One researcher says the new method will prevent natural **phenomena**.
6. T F The researcher believes that the new method will help us make more **informed** responses to natural weather hazards.

Lesson 11

Physiology/Psychology

Dogs and Human Stress

Looking Ahead

As you read today's reading on the next page, look for answers to these questions.

1. What is meant by "olfactory sense"?
2. In what ways have dogs been useful to humans?
3. How do dogs help doctors?
4. What is something that scientists haven't known about people and stress?
5. What questions did an innovative experiment conducted at Queen's University in Belfast, Northern Ireland, try to answer?
6. Who took part in the Queen's University experiment?
7. Why was Clara Wilson encouraged by the results of the experiment?

Part 1 Reading:
Read the essay below and do the activities that follow.

DL 47

[1] Dogs have a powerful sense of smell that humans have taken advantage of for countless millennia. Today, dogs' olfactory sense is **indispensable** in all kinds of practical, life-saving ways. Dogs' amazing noses help us locate lost or missing persons, track down crime **suspects** or escaped prisoners, search for survivors at disaster sites, detect buried land mines, and sniff out illegal drugs at airports. Dogs' remarkable sense of smell is now also aiding doctors in the diagnosis of serious diseases like diabetes and cancer, as well as viral infections such as COVID-19.

[2] Physiological and psychological studies show that humans give off distinctive odors depending on their moods. But scientists haven't known for certain whether people emit a special smell when they experience stress. At the same time, physiologists have wondered whether dogs would be able to recognize that smell, as they can with odors related to other moods and emotions like fear, worry, and happiness. Now, an innovative experiment conducted at Queen's University in Belfast, Northern Ireland, led by PhD candidate Clara Wilson has found that the answer to both these questions is a **gratifying** "yes."

[3] The experiment, reported on Google News, was based on samples of breath and sweat taken from 36 non-smokers. These samples were collected both before and after the participants attempted to work out a challenging math problem that the subjects were pressured into doing very quickly in their heads. The participants' before-and-after heart rates and blood pressures were measured as indicators of stress levels. Four dogs of different breeds that had been trained to use a special detecting device then smelled the samples.

[4] Overall, the dogs successfully detected an odor specifically linked to stress 94.44 percent of the time—that is, in 675 of 720 tries. Research leader Clara Wilson was buoyed up by the study's **outcome**. "Dogs can **discriminate** between breath and sweat samples taken from humans prior to and following a task that **induced** stress," she said. "This **reveals** two important things. The first is that acute, negative, psychological stress changes the odor of people's breath and sweat. The second is that dogs can detect this change." Wilson believes that this new information will have a very important practical application. In particular, it will help improve the training of service dogs that assist people who are suffering from severe anxiety or post-**traumatic** stress disorder, PTSD.

Notes millennia：millennium（千年間）の複数形 / olfactory：嗅覚の / locate：場所を突き止める / track down：追い詰める、追跡する / land mine：地雷 / sniff out：嗅ぎつける / aid：手伝う / diagnosis：診断 / diabetes：糖尿病 / viral infection：ウィルス性感染症 / physiological：生理学の / give off：発する、放出する / distinctive：特徴的な / odor：匂い / for certain：はっきりと、確実に / conduct：行う / PhD candidate：博士候補生 / attempt：試みる / work out：（問題を）解く / subject：被験者 / heart rate：心拍数 / indicator：指標 / breed：品種、血統 / buoy up：元気づける / acute：激しい、深刻な / application：応用 / service dog：介護犬 / post-traumatic stress disorder：心的外傷後ストレス障害（トラウマになる出来事を経験した後に始まる、日常生活に支障をきたす強く不快な反応のこと）

Part 2 Comprehension:

Follow the instructions for each activity below.

A *Complete each sentence below. Listen to check your answers.* DL 48

1. Dogs have been useful to humans for ______________________.
2. Dogs help us look for ______________________

   ______________________.
3. At airports, police use dogs to ______________________.
4. Doctors use dogs to diagnose ______________________

   ______________________.

B *Choose the correct answer.*

5. The word "physiological" refers to
   a. the emotions. b. the body. c. smells.
6. Dogs recognize the particular odors caused by people's different
   a. moods. b. characters. c. ideas.
7. Clara Wilson is studying to become a
   a. philosopher. b. doctor of philosophy. c. dog trainer.

C *Circle T if the sentence is true, F if it is false.*

8. T F In the Queen's University experiment, the researchers allowed the 36 participants to take their time solving the math problems because the problems were so challenging.
9. T F People's heart rates and blood pressures can be used to measure their stress levels.
10. T F The dogs in the experiment had to use a special detecting device that they had not learned to use beforehand.

D ***Writing Challenge:*** *Write a full-sentence answer to each question below. Listen to check your answers.* DL 49

11. What two questions did the Queen's University researchers want to answer?

   ____

   ____
12. What two important things did Clara Wilson say the experiment showed?

   ____

   ____

Part 3 Vocabulary Study: *Follow the instructions for each activity below.*

A *Fill in the blank in each sentence-definition or description below with one of these words. (The words are highlighted in bold in the reading.)*

discriminate	gratifying	indispensable	induce
outcome	reveal	suspect	traumatic

1. A person that the police think has committed a crime is a _______________.
2. When you are able to _______________ between things, you can tell the difference between them.
3. I really need my smartphone. It has become _______________ to me.
4. I was disappointed in the _______________ of my biology experiment. The results were different from what I had hoped for.
5. If I ask you to not _______________ a secret, you should not tell it to anyone.
6. Don't let people _______________ or force you into doing what you don't want to do.
7. A _______________ experience is one that is very distressing or upsetting.
8. When we do a good job at work, we are satisfied and proud, and find it to be very _______________.

B *Fill in the blank in each sentence below with one of these prepositions to make an idiomatic phrase. Listen to check your answers. (The phrase's meaning is shown in brackets after each sentence.)*

DL 50

down	off	out	up

1. The fruit known as durian **gives** __________ a really foul odor. [emit, produce]
2. My neighbors helped me **track** __________ my lost dog. [look for, find]
3. I was **buoyed** __________ by my excellent test scores. [encourage, cheer]
4. I can't **work** __________ the meaning of this acronym. [understand, solve]

Part 4 Listening Challenge: *Read the sentences below. Make sure you understand the words in bold in each sentence. Then listen to the short talk and circle T if each sentence below is true, or F if it is false.*

DL 51

1. T F PTSD most often **afflicts** people who have **witnessed** or experienced a natural disaster like an earthquake or **wildfire**.
2. T F Actually, Clara Wilson was correct about service dogs' being able to help people who **suffer** from PTSD.
3. T F Dogs that serve in the **military** can become **victims** of PTSD, too.
4. T F The loss of an owner through death or **abandonment** is NOT a cause of PTSD in dogs.
5. T F Even the loud noise of a **thunderstorm** or a **fireworks** display can be traumatic for a dog.

Lesson 12

Geophysics/Ornithology

Birds' Magnetic Navigation

Looking Ahead

As you read today's reading on the next page, look for answers to these questions.

1. What is bird migration?
2. What is a bird's "internal compass"?
3. What are some examples of "topographical signposts"?
4. What is Earth's magnetic field? What are some ideas about how birds use that field to navigate?
5. What does "vagrancy" mean when talking about birds?
6. What are some examples of "increased solar activity"?
7. How are light pollution and habitat destruction affecting birds?

Part 1 Reading:
Read the essay below and do the activities that follow. DL 52

[1] Bird migration is the round-trip, often **hazardous** journeys that 4,000 migratory bird species **embark** on every spring and fall. To find their way during these heroic flights, birds employ an internal compass that uses diverse navigational techniques. Birds have acute senses of sight, hearing, and smell that enable them to recognize natural and man-made topographical signposts like mountains, forests, roads, rivers, buildings, towns, and even landfills. During the day, birds navigate by the sun's position in the sky; at night, they use the stars.

[2] Migrating birds also rely on Earth's **invisible** magnetic field, which is generated by the planet's rotation and its liquid-metal core. How exactly birds "see" and use this field is not completely understood, but several **hypotheses** have tried to explain it. One is that magneto-receptors—called cryptochromes—in birds' eyes act like eyeglasses that reveal the magnetic field to them. Another theory is that tiny particles of magnetite in birds' beaks work like a GPS unit.

[3] A recent UCLA ecologists' study shows that Earth's magnetic field can, however, sometimes lead birds astray. They get lost, in other words. This phenomenon is known as "vagrancy." It is attributed to birds' navigational senses being **impaired** when the magnetic field is disturbed by increased solar activity such as sunspots and solar flares. Human-generated radio waves and electronics are also suspected of changing the magnetic field. But when the researchers compared historical data on solar activity with the **incidence** or frequency of vagrancy, they found something very surprising. Increased solar activity (or human devices) did NOT **correlate** with more frequent vagrancies. Such disturbances do make birds' magneto-receptors temporarily inoperable. So what do birds do during those times? They fall back on their other navigating skills.

[4] Radio-wave and electronics interference is just one way that humans make bird migration more difficult and dangerous. Every year, light pollution—artificial lighting that changes natural patterns of light and dark—kills millions of night-flying birds. The birds are lured into collisions with windows and radio towers. Also, the loss of birds' habitats brought on by population growth, land development, and global warming has caused many bird species to **vanish**. One University of Queensland study concludes: "Habitat destruction means that the lifecycles of 90 percent of all migratory birds are poorly protected and thus threatened."

Notes round-trip：往復の / migratory bird：渡り鳥 / employ：用いる、使用する / acute：鋭い / topographical：地形上の / signpost：道標 / landfill：埋立地 / rotation：自転 / magneto-：磁力の、磁気の / receptor：受容体、レセプター / cryptochrome：クリプトクロム（光エネルギーの受容体として働く色素タンパク質のこと）/ particle：小片、粒子 / magnetite：磁鉄鉱 / beak：くちばし / unit：装置一式 / UCLA：カリフォルニア大学ロサンゼルス校（University of California, Los Angeles）/ ecologist：生態学者 / astray：道をはずれて / vagrancy：放浪、流浪 / attribute A to B：A を B に帰する / disturb：乱す / sunspot：太陽黒点 / solar flare：太陽フレア / radio wave：電波 / suspect A of B：A に B の嫌疑をかける / inoperable：実行できない、機能しない / fall back on：～に頼る / lure：おびき寄せる / collision：衝突 / habitat：生息地 / bring on：引き起こす、もたらす

Part 2 Comprehension:
Follow the instructions for each activity below.

A *Write a short answer to each question below. Listen to check your answers.* DL 53

1. When do birds migrate?

____

2. What are birds' "internal compass" made up of?

____

3. What are some examples of "topographical signposts"?

____

4. How do migrating birds navigate at night?

____

B *Circle T if the sentence is true, F if it is false.*

5. T F The way birds use the earth's magnetic field to navigate is still something of a mystery to scientists.
6. T F The magneto-receptors in a bird's eyes are in a way like eyeglasses that allow them to see Earth's magnetic field.
7. T F "Cryptochromes" in the birds' beaks act like a GPS unit.

C *Fill in the blanks in the sentences below. Listen to check your answers.* DL 54

8. The phenomenon known as vagrancy comes when birds' ____________ senses don't work correctly. The ____________ field has been disturbed by increased ____________ activity.
9. ____________ radio waves and electronics can also cause birds' magneto-receptors to become temporarily ____________.
10. In such cases, ____________ birds use other navigational ____________.

D ***Writing Challenge:*** *Write a full-sentence answer to each question below. Listen to check your answers.* DL 55

11. How does light pollution lead to the deaths of millions of birds each year?

____

____

12. What are the main causes of the destruction of birds' habitats?

____

____

Part 3 Vocabulary Study: Follow the instructions for each activity below.

A *Match these KEY WORDS from today's reading with their definitions and synonyms below. Write the words on the lines. (The words are highlighted in bold in the reading.)*

correlate embark hazardous hypotheses impair incidences invisible vanish

1. ________________ a. ideas about why things happen; theories
2. ________________ b. happenings; occurrences
3. ________________ c. to damage or make weak; harm; lessen
4. ________________ d. to set out on a journey; start something new
5. ________________ e. to disappear completely; go extinct; die out
6. ________________ f. to place two things together to compare them
7. ________________ g. very dangerous; perilous
8. ________________ h. unable to be seen; undetectable

B *Rewrite each sentence below by replacing the underline part with one of these phrases. Make the necessary changes. Listen to check your sentences.*

DL 56

(be) led astray fall back on (be) lured into be suspected of

1. Joe was tempted to skip school by one of his classmates.

____

2. I got lost because my smartphone gave me the wrong directions.

____

3. The teacher thought I had cheated, but I had written the essay myself.

____

4. I was out of a job and had to use my savings to get by.

____

Part 4 Listening Challenge: As you listen to the short talk, fill in each blank below. Listen again to check your answers.

DL 57

Why do birds migrate? The reasons are quite simple. The main reason is to get better ____________ to food. Another is to escape the ____________ temperatures, strong ____________, and snowstorms of northern ____________. In a nutshell, migration increases the birds' and their ____________ (that is, their babies') chances of ____________.

How do birds know when it is time to take off? Ornithologists believe that birds have an ____________ clock. The clock starts ticking due to gradual changes in ____________ lengths, ____________ in temperature, and ____________ food supplies. Birds' ____________ may also put out a special ____________ that tells them it is time to go.

Lesson 13

Engineering/Medicine

3-D Homes and Hearts

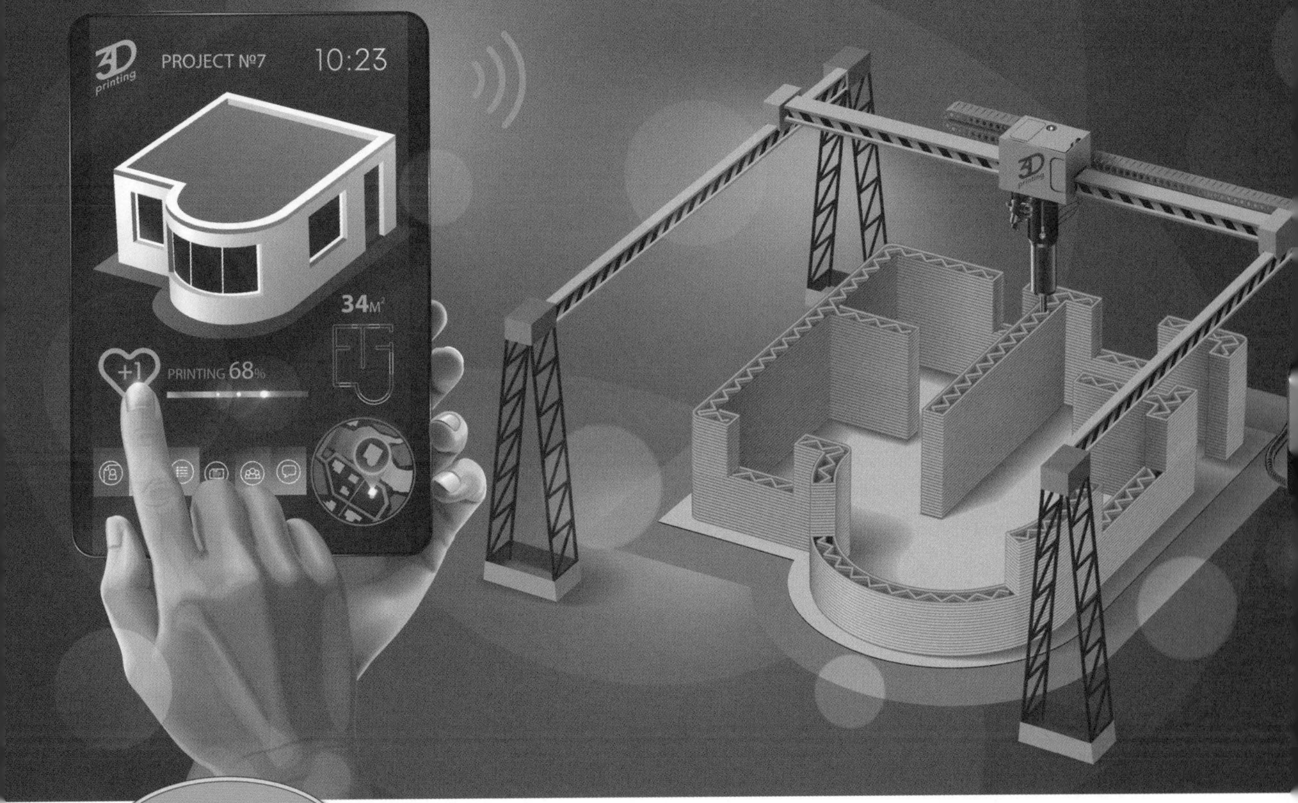

Looking Ahead

As you read today's reading on the next page, look for answers to these questions.

1. Who is Jason Ballard? What is he committed to?
2. What problems make the world's housing shortage worse?
3. How does the 3-D-printing building-construction process work?
4. Why is that process more customer friendly?
5. What is Habitat for Humanity? What has it done recently?
6. What is happening in Mexico and Dubai regarding 3-D-printing building construction?
7. How, according to one *New Yorker* writer, will 3-D-printing construction help "expand human habitation beyond Earth"?

Part 1 Reading:

Read the essay below and do the activities that follow.

DL 58

[1] "There are far too many homeless people. Working-class people can't afford basic housing. Construction is too wasteful. Houses aren't energy efficient ... We are the most advanced version of humanity that has ever existed. And yet, we can't even meet this basic human need properly. Future housing can't—not shouldn't, but *can't*—be like today's housing." These **ardent** words come from entrepreneur Jason Ballard, as quoted by the *New Yorker*'s Rachel Monroe. Ballard is **committed** to helping solve the world's housing crisis, a problem that is **exacerbated** by supply and labor issues, high-priced construction materials, and social ills like discrimination and inequality.

[2] Ballard, along with a partner, set up a construction company called Icon in 2017. He **swears** that the solution lies with 3-D-printed construction. This is an automated method that **erects** buildings layer by layer using cement-based material. It does this faster, more cheaply, and in a more ecologically sustainable and customer-friendly way. It allows homebuyers to easily and economically—without taking on a high-priced architect—customize their homes. No wonder the method is catching on. America's first fully 3-D-printed home was unveiled in Austin, Texas, in 2018. In December 2021, a Virginia family moved into a two-story, 1,200-square-foot, three-bedroom 3-D-printed home that had been built by the non-profit charity organization, Habitat for Humanity. The house was put up in just 12 hours, compared to at least a month with conventional construction. The cost? A **paltry** $10,000.

[3] More and more countries are **embracing** the trend. An entire 3-D-printed neighborhood is now under construction in Mexico. It will provide 50 new weather-resistant homes to low-income families in a poverty-stricken area subject to natural catastrophes. Dubai, which already boasts the world's largest 3-D-printed office complex, has pledged that by 2030, one-fourth of all its new buildings will be 3-D-printing constructed.

[4] "3-D printing has also **emerged** as a promising way to build the landing pads, roads, and other infrastructure needed to expand human habitation beyond Earth," says Rachel Monroe. In fact, NASA recently launched a program called 3-D-Printed Habitat Challenge that aims to enable us to build 3-D-printed homes for colonists on Mars.

***NOTE:** Today's Listening Challenge discusses another type of 3-D printing.*

Notes working-class：労働者階級の / basic：（必要とされる）最低レベルの / entrepreneur：企業家 / quote：引用する / material：材料 / social ills：社会悪 / discrimination：偏見 / take on：雇う / catch on：人気を博する / unveil：発表する / two-story：２階建ての / 1,200-square-foot：1,200 平方フィートの / put up：（建物などを）建てる / neighborhood：地域、地区 / weather-resistant：厳しい気象条件に耐える、耐候性の / -stricken：（病気・災難・悲しみなどに）襲われた、打ちひしがれた / subject to：～を受けやすい、左右される / catastrophe：大災害、大惨事 / Dubai：ドバイ（アラブ首長国連邦北東部の首長国、及びその首都）/ boast：～を誇りとする / pledge：～を誓う / landing pad：ヘリコプター着陸所 / colonist：植民者

Part 2 Comprehension:
Follow the instructions for each activity below.

A *Write short answers to each question below. Listen to check your answers.*

1. What does Jason Ballard say that people today are?

____

2. What two things does Ballard say are wrong with housing today?

____

3. What problem is Ballard working to help solve?

____

4. What two social problems contribute to the global housing crisis?

____

B *Circle T if the sentence is true, F if it is false.*

5. T F When he established his construction company Icon in 2017, Ballard did it completely on his own.
6. T F Unlike most traditional homes, most 3-D-printed homes are constructed of an artificial plastic-based material.
7. T F With 3-D-printed homes, home-buyers can save time and money by not having to use a professional architect.
8. T F Usually, constructing a two-story, three-bedroom family home would take a month or more.

C *Fill in the blanks in the sentences below.*

9. The homes in Mexico are being built in a ________________ area that has frequent ________________. They will belong to ________________ families.
10. Dubai has ________________ that by 2030, ________________ percent of all its new buildings will be ________________.

D ***Writing Challenge:*** *Write a full-sentence answer to each question below. Listen to check your answers.* DL 59

11. What most likely is the primary purpose and/or function of Habitat for Humanity?

____

12. Based on what you know about Jason Ballard, what can you say about his character? What kind of person is he?

____

Part 3 Vocabulary Study: Follow the instructions for each activity below.

A *Fill in the blank in each sentence-definition or description below with one of these words. (The words are highlighted in bold in the reading.)*

ardent	committed	embrace	emerge
erect	exacerbate	paltry	swear

1. Things that ______________ a social problem make the problem worse.
2. When you ______________ that you will do something, you promise to do it.
3. An ______________ person does most things with enthusiasm and passion.
4. A good but formal synonym for the verb "build" is ______________.
5. Cicadas ______________ or come out from uderground every ten years.
6. If you make a ______________ wage at work, you don't make much money.
7. When you are ______________ to losing weight, you are determined to do it.
8. ______________ means to hug, but it also means to accept an idea or belief.

B *Rewrite each short sentence below by substituting one of these phrasal verbs for the underlined part. Make any necessary changes. Listen to check your sentences.*

DL 60

catch on	put up	set up	take on

1. We are building a fence to keep wild deer out of our yard.

   ____

2. Establishing a start-up company takes know-how, guts, and money.

   ____

3. Our restaurant recently hired several bilingual servers.

   ____

4. The new chatbot has really become popular with university students.

   ____

Part 4 Listening Challenge: Read the sentences below. Make sure you understand the word(s) in bold in each sentence. Then listen to the short talk and circle T if each sentence below is true, or F if it is false.

DL 61

1. T F Every day, 70 Americans die waiting for an **organ transplant**.
2. T F **Kidneys** are the most-needed organs.
3. T F In all, each year, only 14,000 organs are **donated** in the U.S.
4. T F If you want to be a **donor** yourself, you must sign up to do it.
5. T F It is quite easy to **match recipients** with donated organs.
6. T F **3-D bioprinting** technology is still being developed.

Lesson 14

Biometric Technology

Facial Recognition, Friend or Foe?

Looking Ahead

As you read today's reading on the next page, look for answers to these questions.

1. What is facial-recognition technology?
2. Why is the technology so controversial these days?
3. How many steps are involved in the facial-recognition process?
4. What are some of the most important *useful* applications of the software?
5. To what kinds of purposes does *Forbes* magazine say that facial-recognition technology is being used?
6. Who is most frequently guilty of abusing facial-recognition technology?
7. For what purposes are Iran, China, and Israel using the technology?

Part 1 Reading:
Read the essay below and do the activities that follow. DL 62

[1] Facial-recognition software, an advanced form of biometrics, is used to confirm people's identities. This function—because of today's **profound** concerns about privacy and human-rights **violations**—makes facial recognition one of the most controversial of all modern technologies, on a par, perhaps, with genetic editing/engineering.

[2] Although different facial-recognition systems exist, they all work the same for the most part. Step 1: An AI-equipped camera locates a face. Step 2: The camera takes a photo (image) of the face. Step 3: The software analyzes or "reads" the face's "topography." Step 4: The image is converted into a mathematical equation, known as a faceprint, that contains all the face's unique data. Step 5: A special program compares the faceprint to photos in a huge database and keeps on looking until it finds a match.

[3] Facial recognition is not by any means only controversial. It has many practical, vital uses: passport control at airports; crime detection and prevention; searching for missing or **abducted** persons; **expediting** hospital care; making banking transactions more efficient and secure. But the problem is that the technology is also used for "**sinister** purposes," says *Forbes* magazine. These uses, or, rather, abuses, are almost always **perpetrated** in the name of security, convenience, and efficiency. And those abuses are why the technology makes headlines almost every day.

[4] Governments are often the culprits. Iran now uses facial recognition to identify—and then punish or imprison—women who do not **conform** to the country's strict hijab dress code. Israel uses the technology to keep an eye on Palestinians living in the West Bank. China employs the software to "profile" ethnic minorities and then uses the data to harass, track, detain, and generally mistreat them. A recent BBC report says that police departments all across the United States and in the United Kingdom are also abusing facial recognition by inputting false data into the system. This can lead to innocent people being arrested. Australia is now using facial recognition at casinos to keep out "problem" gamblers, **ostensibly** to help people get over their addiction. But civil rights groups say "the tech is ineffective for stopping problem gambling and could be used for wider surveillance."

NOTE: *The conclusion to this passage appears in today's Listening Challenge.*

Notes biometrics：生物測定学、生体認証 / confirm：確かめる / controversial：論議の的となる / on a par with：～と同様で、同等で / locate：～の位置を捜し当てる / topography：形状的な諸特徴とその構造的な関係、形態 / convert：変える / not by any means：決して～ではない / vital：重要な / detection：検出 / abuse：悪用 / culprit：犯罪者 / imprison：投獄する / hijab：ヒジャーブ（イスラム教徒の女性が人前で顔を隠すのに用いるかぶりもの）/ Palestinians：パレスチナ人 / West Bank：ヨルダン川西岸地区（ユダヤ人とパレスチナ人が居住している場所。それぞれ居住エリアが決められていて、生活は分離されている）/ ethnic：民族の / harass：苦しめる / track：追跡する / detain：拘留する / mistreat：虐待する / innocent：無実の / keep out：締め出す / addiction：依存、中毒 / surveillance：監視

Part 2 Comprehension:
Follow the instructions for each activity below.

A *Choose the correct answer.*

1. Which of these is NOT mentioned in paragraph 1 as something that people today are concerned about?

   a. privacy b. human rights c. mental health

2. In paragraph 1, what is implied about facial recognition?

   a. It may be more dangerous than genetic engineering.

   b. More people use it than use genetic engineering.

   c. It is probably as controversial as genetic engineering.

B *Briefly answer each question below. Listen to check your answers.* DL 63

3. What is facial recognition used for at airports?

   ____

4. How does facial recognition help the police?

   ____

5. Who can facial recognition help find?

   ____

C *Circle T if the sentence is true, F if it is false.*

6. T F So far, facial recognition has no applications in medicine.
7. T F *Forbes* thinks that facial recognition should never be used.
8. T F The word "culprits" as used in paragraph 4 means "wrongdoers."
9. T F Some police departments in the U.S. and the U.K. are using facial recognition in an illegal way.
10. T F Facial recognition, according to civil rights groups, is an excellent way to solve the problem of gambling addiction.

D ***Writing Challenge:*** *Follow the instructions for each activity below.* DL 64

11. Reread paragraph 2 about how facial recognition works. Then, explain the process by briefly writing out each step. Listen to check your answers.

    Step 1: ______________________________

    Step 2: ______________________________

    Step 3: ______________________________

    Step 4: ______________________________

    Step 5: ______________________________

12. Write an answer to this question. Listen to check your sentence.

    What excuse do people who abuse facial recognition offer for using it?

    ____

Part 3 Vocabulary Study: *Follow the instructions for each activity below.*

A *Match these KEY WORDS from today's reading with their definitions and synonyms below. Write the words on the lines. (The words are highlighted in bold in the reading.)*

abduct	conform	expedite	ostensibly
perpetrate	profound	sinister	violation

1. ____________________ a. deep; very serious; sincere; intense
2. ____________________ b. apparently but not actually; in name only
3. ____________________ c. to capture a person illegally; kidnap
4. ____________________ d. the breaking of a rule or law; crime
5. ____________________ e. commit a crime; carry out an illegal action
6. ____________________ f. to adhere; obey; stick to a rule
7. ____________________ g. to speed up; make faster; accelerate
8. ____________________ h. evil; wicked; malicious

B *Fill in the blank in each sentence below with one of these common idiomatic phrases. [The phrase's meaning is given in brackets.] Listen to check your answers.* DL 65

for the most part [generally; usually; by and large]
keep an eye on [watch; look at carefully]
(not) by any means [in no way; absolutely not; not at all]
on a par with [equal to]

1. Will you ____________________ my dog Sam while I'm away on vacation?
2. Thai cuisine is ____________________ too spicy for my taste.
3. If you ask me, Japanese baseball is now ____________________ American baseball.
4. I would ____________________ say anything to offend or hurt you.

Part 4 Listening Challenge: *Listen to the short talk. Then listen to the sentences about the talk. Circle T below if the sentence you hear is true, or F if it is false.* DL 66

1. T F 2. T F 3. T F 4. T F
5. T F 6. T F 7. T F 8. T F

Lesson 15

Everyday Science and Technology (3)

Science Writing: A World of Learning

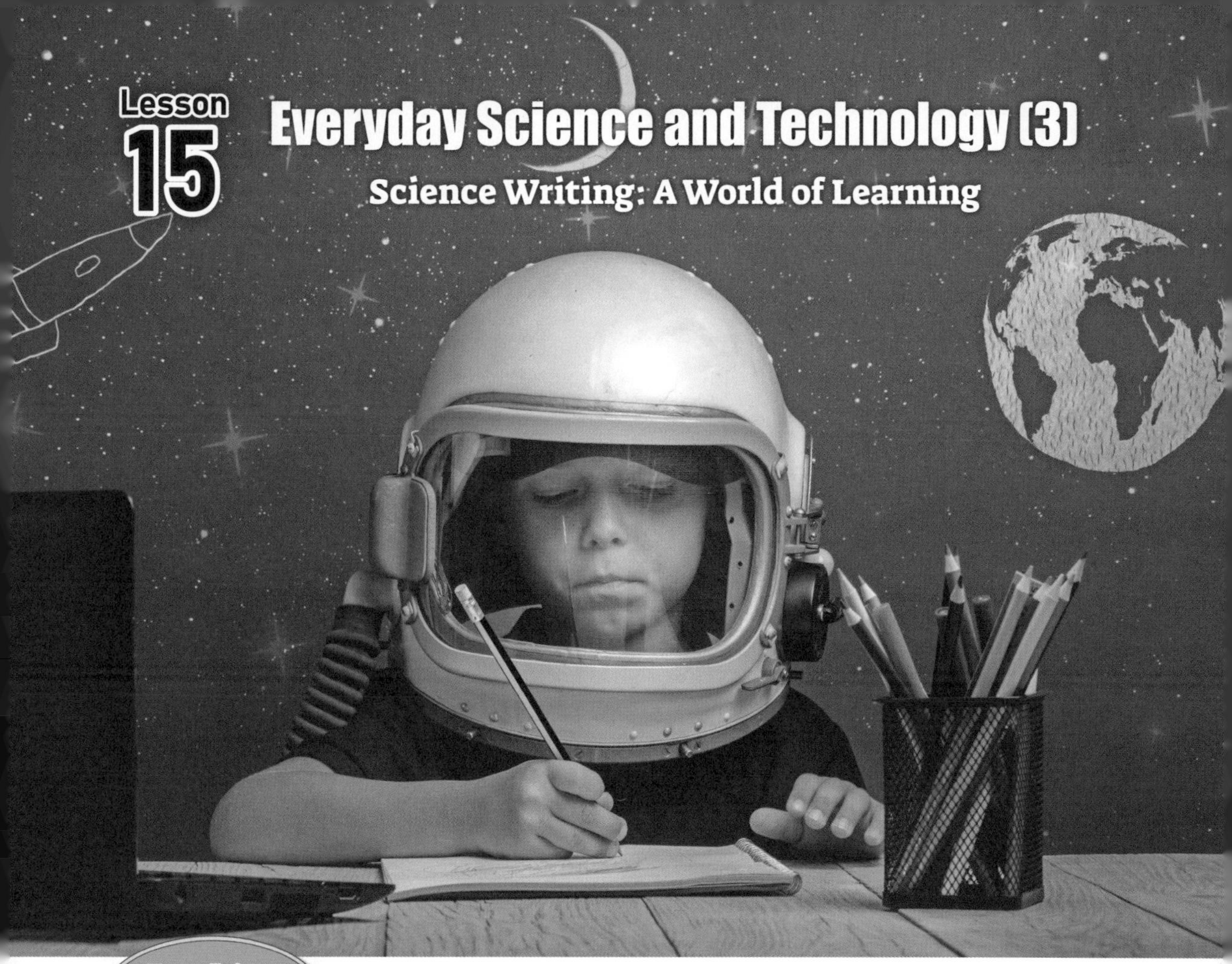

Looking Ahead

As you read today's reading on the next page, look for answers to these questions.

1. What is the goal of popular-science writing?
2. What makes popular-science authors such interesting writers?
3. Who is Ed Yong? What is the name of his latest book?
4. What does Yong's book show us or take us into?
5. What examples does Yong give of different animal species' ways of experiencing the world?
6. What is David Quammen's most recent book called? What is it about?
7. What had many virologists warned prior to the onset of the COVID-19 pandemic?
8. What idea did Quammen's book "debunk"?

Part 1 Reading:
Read the essay below and do the activities that follow.

DL 67

[1] The goal of popular-science writing is to make science (and technology) accessible and interesting to lay (that is, non-professional) readers. Most popular-science writers are scientists who also love writing and have a wonderful way with words. They **endeavor** to persuade us to see the world with open eyes and through the lens of science. Ed Yong is an **acclaimed**, Pulitzer-Prize-winning science journalist. “The best science writing **illuminates** connections between us and the rest of the world,” Yong believes.

[2] In his *An Immense World: How Animal Senses Reveal the Hidden Realms Around Us*, Yong **accomplishes** that and much more. The book’s main topic is summed up in the introduction: “Earth teems with sights and textures, sounds and vibrations, smells and tastes. But every animal can tap into only a small fraction of reality’s fullness.” In *An Immense World*, Yong opens up the lives of hundreds of animals. He shows us how each species deals with this “small fraction” in its own unique way. Catfish, Yong tells us, for example, have “teeth and tastebuds spread across their entire bodies.” Scallops’ shells are lined with eyes—“dozens of eyes in some species and up to 200 in others.” Crickets have ears in their knees. Many fish species produce their own electricity. *An Immense World* is “full of such little astonishments,” says the *New York Times*, and should be read slowly and carefully, inspiring us to experience the world with “awe and wonder.”

[3] Another fascinating recent popular-science book is *Breathless: The Scientific Race to Defeat a Deadly Virus* by veteran non-fiction author David Quammen. It also calls for slow, close reading, but for different reasons. It is an admonishment. That “deadly virus” in the title is, of course, COVID-19. Before its outbreak, virologists and infectious disease scientists had warned for decades that a pandemic stemming from a virus “spilling over” from a nonhuman source was a **dreadful** possibility. And then it actually came about, almost overnight, it now seems. Quammen’s book reads like a great detective story. It is a **meticulous** investigation to discover the origins of COVID-19. It **debunks** the now tossed-out theory that the virus somehow “escaped” from a mysterious research laboratory in China. *Breathless* winds up with another warning: “COVID-19 won’t be our last pandemic. It probably won’t be our worst.”

***NOTE:** Several more popular science books are introduced in today’s Listening Challenge.*

Notes lay：素人の / have a way with：～の扱い方を知っている / persuade：説得する / Pulitzer Prize：ピューリッツァー賞（毎年ジャーナリズム・文学・音楽などで功績のある米国人に与えられる賞）/ teem with：～で満ちている / texture：触感 / fraction：破片、断片、小部分 / catfish：ナマズ / tastebud：味蕾 / scallop：ホタテガイ / cricket：コオロギ / awe：畏敬、畏怖 / veteran：経験豊富な、ベテランの / call for：～を要求する / admonishment：勧告、忠告、警告 / outbreak：（伝染病などの）急激な発生 / virologist：ウィルス学者 / pandemic：流行病 / spill：こぼれる / come about：起こる、生ずる / overnight：一夜のうちに出現した、突然の / tossed-out：放棄された / wind up with：～で終わる

Part 2 Comprehension:

Follow the instructions for each activity below.

A *Choose the correct answer.*

1. Another word for "non-professional" used in paragraph 1 is
   a. lay. b. amateur. c. hack.
2. How do science writers want us to see the world?
   a. more openly b. more scientifically c. both a. and b.
3. What is implied about why popular-science authors make such excellent writers?
   a. They are all famous scientists.
   b. They are exceptionally intelligent.
   c. They know how to use words well.

B *Circle T if the sentence is true, F if it is false.*

4. T F The underlined pronoun "that" at the beginning of paragraph 2 refers to what good science writing does.
5. T F The term "small fraction of reality's fullness" as used in paragraph 2 refers to an animal's own habitat or living space.
6. T F Crickets have up to 200 ears in their knees.
7. T F The *New York Times* says that *An Immense World* should be read quickly in one sitting.

C *Complete each sentence below. Listen to check your answers.* DL 68

8. David Quammen is ______________________.
9. *Breathless* also demands ______________________.
10. Virologists warned that a virus might ______________________.

D ***Writing Challenge:*** *Write a full-sentence answer to each question below. Listen to check your answers.* DL 69

11. What makes the author say that *Breathless* reads in a way like a detective story?

____

____

12. Why might *Breathless* be considered a pessimistic or even scary book?

____

____

Part 3 Vocabulary Study: Follow the instructions for each activity below.

A *Match these KEY WORDS from today's reading with their definitions and synonyms below. Write the words on the lines. (The words are highlighted in bold in the reading.)*

acclaimed	accomplish	debunk	dreadful
endeavor	illuminate	immense	meticulous

1. ____________________ a. to try very hard; make a great effort
2. ____________________ b. to do something important; achieve
3. ____________________ c. to explain; reveal; shed light on
4. ____________________ d. very careful; fastidious; diligent
5. ____________________ e. huge; enormous
6. ____________________ f. very frightening; horrible; terrible
7. ____________________ g. highly praised; admired; applauded
8. ____________________ h. to prove false or exaggerated; disprove

B *Replace the underlined word or phrase in each sentence below with one of these phrasal verbs from today's reading. Write the phrase in the brackets.*

call for	stem from	tap into	toss out	sum up	wind up

1. You have talent. You should make use of [ ] it.
2. Your problems are caused by [ ] your negative attitude.
3. Summarize [ ] the book's main idea in one sentence.
4. These recipes require [ ] too much butter and salt.
5. Be careful, or you will become [ ] sick.
6. I never discard [ ] my old school textbooks.

Part 4 Listening Challenge: Listen to the short talk about several new popular-science books. Then match these authors with their books. Write the letters on the lines in front of the book titles.

DL 70

a. Matthew Ball **b.** Riley Black **c.** Lars Chittka
d. Sarah Everts **e.** Greta Thunberg

1. ________ *The Mind of a Bee*
2. ________ *The Climate Book*
3. ________ *The Joy of Sweat*
4. ________ *The Metaverse, and How It Will Revolutionize Everything*
5. ________ *The Last Days of the Dinosaurs*

Everyday Science and Technology—News You Can Use [B-960]
日常生活にみる現代の科学技術を読む

1刷 2024年1月22日

著　者	ジム・カヌーセン　Jim Knudsen
注釈者	佐竹　幸信　Yukinobu Satake
発行者	南雲　一範　Kazunori Nagumo
発行所	株式会社　南雲堂 〒162-0801　東京都新宿区山吹町361 NAN'UN-DO Co., Ltd. 361 Yamabuki-cho, Shinjuku-ku, Tokyo 162-0801, Japan 振替口座：00160-0-46863 TEL:　03-3268-2311（営業部：学校関係） 03-3268-2384（営業部：書店関係） 03-3268-2387（編集部） FAX:　03-3269-2486
編集者	加藤　敦
組　版	柴崎　利恵
装　丁	銀月堂
検　印	省　略
コード	ISBN978-4-523-17960-3　C0082

Printed in Japan

E-mail : nanundo@post.email.ne.jp
URL : https://www.nanun-do.co.jp/

Pencil drawing by Jim Knudsen